LAWYERS AND LAWSUITS:

A Guide to Litigation

by Robert A. Izard

MACMILLAN SPECTRUM

An imprint of Macmillan • USA
A Simon & Schuster Macmillan Company
1633 Broadway
New York, NY 10019-6785

The legal system is often a mystery, and we, its priests, preside over rituals baffling to everyday citizens.

—Henry G. Miller

This book is dedicated to my clients who have helped me learn to explain the litigation process in clear, simple language.

A Spectrum Book

MACMILLAN and SPECTRUM are registered trademarks of Macmillan, Inc.

10   9   8   7   6   5   4   3   2   1

ISBN: 0-02861616-2
Library of Congress Number: 96-078164

The stories, anecdotes, examples, characters, names, incidents, and statements in this book are fiction or used fictionally. Any resemblance to actual persons or events is purely coincidental.

This book does not give, is not intended to give and should not be construed to give legal advice. Anyone in need of legal advice should consult an attorney.

Manufactured in the United States of America

CONTENTS

INTRODUCTION

Litigation is becoming a national pastime. The trials of O.J. Simpson and the "Nanny" were a focal point for the media and millions of TV viewers. Novels and movies on legal issues appear monthly. Civil litigation affects the lives of many Americans. "I'll see you in court!" is an all-too-familiar response to disputes.

Yet, few non-lawyers understand the litigation process or the dynamics involved. For many caught up in a lawsuit, litigation is like being on a train hurtling down the tracks. This train may be driven by a lawyer they barely know and may not fully trust. Those involved often feel like victims of a process they do not understand and that doesn't appear to further their goals. They may not know why a lawyer does what he does or whether he is doing a good or bad job. Because many litigants are unaware of the "ins and outs," they cannot always ensure that lawsuits are pursued solely to achieve the results they desire.

Similarly, many who follow lawsuits on television and in the press do not understand litigation. Media coverage is often incomplete and inaccurate. The press rarely gives a context in which to consider and analyze legal issues and strategies. Rather, ratings and "headline reporting" encourage attention only to the most dramatic aspects of a case. For reasons beyond their control, the public and media remain so uneducated about the litigation process that they cannot responsibly evaluate it.

Lawyers and Lawsuits: A Guide to Litigation is a lively, readable analysis of the litigation process, including its underlying dynamics and interests. Through true-life illustrations, it provides the context vital to anyone hoping to understand and evaluate lawsuits. It explains not only what should and should not happen during a lawsuit, but why. It examines the factors that drive litigation in the context of all events that might occur.

Lawyers and Lawsuits is not, however, a nuts-and-bolts, step-by-step guide on how to prosecute a lawsuit. It gives you a big-picture view. With this book, you will see what goes on in litigation and why. You will have the tools to evaluate your lawyers and lawsuits. You can ensure that the litigation process works for you. You will save time and money in resolving your disputes.

Some contend that lawyers are running the legal system and that the system is out of control. *Lawyers and Lawsuits* will enable you to understand the system and see where the litigation train is going. More important, you will discover when, where, and how you can end the journey—or why you might want to stay on board.

ACKNOWLEDGMENTS

Many people helped me a great deal in writing this book. Lawyers in the Boston, Hartford, and Stamford offices of Robinson & Cole provided many of the stories and anecdotes, including Earl Phillips, John Tannenbaum, Michael Lurie, Michael Enright, Joe Clasen, Jim Wade, Chris Hug, and Ed Hennessey. I also want to thank mediator Don Reder and Judge George Hodges for their contributions.

I also appreciate the efforts of many people who read drafts of the book. They include lawyers at Robinson & Cole, other lawyers around the country, a judge, clients, and friends. Because of their diverse backgrounds, their contributions have lead to what I hope is a balanced perspective. In particular, I want to thank Jim Hayssen, Dennis Richey, Karen Holton, Fred Boling, Jay Silver, Dick Pundt, Judge George Hodges, Linda O'Connell, Pat Campanella, and Tom Sargant.

Also of great help was Andrew Pope, my agent at Curtis Brown in New York. If you want to write a book, get an agent, because they can open doors that you probably can't on your own.

Particular thanks go to Sandy Paisley, my secretary, who put in lots of time and effort to help whip this book into shape. And finally, I want to thank Susan, Catherine, Thomas, and Margaret, whose love, creativity, and spirit inspired me to write *Lawyers and Lawsuits: A Guide to Litigation*.

WHAT IS A LAWSUIT?

Dennis Williamson knew that his joint venture needed more money to develop an amusement park. He wanted to get it all from his partner, Middleton Investments. Dennis claimed that Middleton invested only $750,000 of the $1,000,000 originally promised. Middleton said it owed nothing and was even entitled to a credit for development services. When they tried to negotiate, Middleton adamantly stated that it would put in more money only if Dennis put in the same amount. Neither made any concessions to the other, and negotiations deteriorated. Dennis then filed a lawsuit to try to threaten Middleton into funding the project. When Middleton refused to back down, they embarked on a costly, four-year litigation which began because they could not discuss rationally a simple money issue. Moreover, because of the hostility created by the lawsuit, they destroyed what could have been a prosperous joint venture. Rather than work together to develop a thriving business, Dennis and Middleton chose to devote their time and effort to the litigation drama.

> "The judicial system is the most expensive machine ever invented for finding out what happened and what to do about it."
>
> —Irving R. Kaufman

A lawsuit is the last resort for those who can't or won't resolve disputes by other nonviolent means. It is time-consuming, expensive, inefficient and often unpredictable. Yet, because many Americans seem unable to resolve disputes outside a courtroom, lawsuits continue.

Every day we resolve disputes. We disagree with our spouses, our children, our friends, our employers, our co-workers and our business contacts. We solve virtually all of these problems in a calm, consensual, conciliatory manner. Only when the dispute becomes sufficiently large and at least one side becomes sufficiently unreasonable and unwilling or unable to understand the other does a lawsuit arise. When we can't work out a problem between ourselves, we need someone else to tell us who is right and who is wrong. Litigation is one of the final problem solvers.

A lawsuit begins when the plaintiff, the party making the claim, files a complaint in court. The suit invariably says that the defendant, the person who gets sued, did something wrong and should pay money or suffer some other penalty. The defendant files a written answer to the claim, usually by denying liability. From this point forward, all action in the litigation drama leads to the trial, where the judge or jury watches the presentations of the parties and ultimately decides right and wrong.

A Play in Two Acts

A trial is in many respects a morality play. In this play, the plaintiff and the defendant each present to the jury their versions of the truth. This "truth" unfolds for the jury as the witnesses and lawyers show and tell the story of what happened. The plaintiff and defendant are the stars. Other witnesses are the supporting cast. The lawyers are sometimes actors and sometimes the directors. The judge is not only an actor but also a director and, at times, the audience. The jury remains always the audience.

> "OK, it's smoke and mirrors. So what? You'd be surprised how much of the legal process is exactly that. Just like in Hollywood, image is everything in the courtroom, Dahhling."
>
> —Darlene Ricker

The litigation play has two acts. Each side directs and produces one of them. The plaintiff presents Act One. His witnesses testify about his version of what happened, hopefully in a way that helps him. The plaintiff may also present documents for the jury to read, pictures for the jury to see, videotapes for the jury to watch and other facts which help his case. At different points throughout Act One, the defendant challenges the plaintiff's presentation with questions to the plaintiff's witnesses and about different documents, pictures and videotapes. Through this cross-examination, the defendant's lawyer attempts to induce the jury to reject Act One in favor of the upcoming Act Two.

In Act Two, the defendant produces and directs the presentation of her version of the truth. Different witnesses, testimony, documents, pictures and videotapes may be presented. Witnesses may also discuss the same documents and pictures from Act One but in a different light. Through this process, the defendant tries to "spin" the case her way. Of course, the plaintiff's lawyer cross-examines the defendant's witnesses to undercut their spin and attempts to reinforce for the jury that Act One is the "real truth."

The Productions Are Biased

The trial process assumes that the parties are not open and balanced in their productions for the jury. Both sides will emphasize facts which help them and ignore or downplay all other facts. Since the participants try to convince the jury to see the case their way, the jury should not rely solely upon either performance but should question and challenge everything that it hears and sees.

The Play Is Adversarial

The litigation play is, by definition, hostile. Lawyers and clients refer to lawsuits as wars they will win by crushing the opposition. In this battle, the defendant and the plaintiff each attack the other's version of what happened. In theory, each side is equally able to present its case in the best way possible. In theory, each side is equally able to challenge and undermine the opposition. In theory, the jury can sift through the conflicting presentations and reach a fair and just decision.

A Lawsuit Should Be Fair

Because it is adversarial, an overriding goal of litigation is to guarantee a fair trial. Fairness dictates that each party have a full and equal opportunity to present its case. In order for the process to be reliable, each side may present virtually anything that it believes supports its claims; this right ensures that the jury has all of the information needed to make a just decision.

To create a level playing field, both parties to the lawsuit may retain a lawyer to represent them. A licensed, trained professional, the lawyer helps clients navigate through the litigation process. The lawyer also enables each party to produce a professional, persuasive act in the play and effectively challenge the opponent's performance.

Discovery and Fairness

Fairness requires that each side be allowed to engage in a pretrial process known as discovery. Discovery consists of the depositions and document productions that can take years and cost huge amounts of money before trial. In this process, the parties "discover" each fact that relates in any way to the other side's case. In discovery, no stone is left unturned. By the time the trial starts, the lawyers and their clients should know all of the facts the jury will learn. They may also learn additional wrongful acts by their opponent. By the time the trial starts, the parties should know each side's version of the truth.

Having learned all of the facts in discovery, each side is better able to produce the most persuasive drama possible and effectively challenge the weak points in the other side's argument. Discovery gives everyone the opportunity to take his best shot. Because of discovery, the jury is theoretically more able to glean the truth from the more thorough and complete performances of the parties.

Lawsuits Are Not Always About the Truth

In many respects, the theory underlying litigation is not the reality. First and foremost, litigation is not always a search for the truth. First and foremost, it is an attempt by the combatants to persuade the jury that their respective conflicting stories are correct. Truth itself is not the issue because a jury cannot always know what really happened.

> "We've produced a system of ending disputes rather than digging up truths."
>
> —Thomas H. Allen

Since trials usually occur many years after the events that are the subject of the lawsuit, and since no juror actually witnessed what happened, the decision of the jury must be based solely on the two-act play. No juror saw, heard, felt, or has any first-hand knowledge of anything that relates to the case. The only information on which the jury relies in deciding right and wrong is second-hand. The information comes solely from the witnesses, pictures, and documents presented at trial. Consequently, the jury's ability to find the "truth" is limited by the abilities of the witnesses to remember the facts and the lawyers and witnesses to present them in a clear, convincing way.

The jury's angle on the "truth" is like a father's view of a fight between his two children. Each child claims that the other hit first. The father did not see the fight. He only knows what his children tell him. In figuring out who hit whom first, he considers many factors, including the personalities of the children, their relative ages, who hit whom first in the past, who tells the truth more often, and who gives the most convincing presentation. Sometimes he relies only on the looks in his children's eyes that he has often seen in the past. Many times the father cannot determine the truth and sends both kids to their rooms.

The jury has bigger problems than the father. First, it has a duty to decide who is right and who is wrong. It can't simply send the plaintiff and defendant to their rooms if it can't make up its mind. Though hung juries occur, the judge will pressure the jury to agree on a winner and a loser.

Second, the jury knows less about the actors and directors in the courtroom drama than the parent knows about his children. For example, the jury knows relatively little about how the actors sound when they are "stretching" the truth, whether they've "hit first" in the past, or what their reputations for truthfulness are. The jurors may not be able to look a witness in the eye and know what happened. Therefore, the jury is less able than the father to see through the acting.

Finally, the play produced in court usually occurs many years after the dispute arises. In contrast, the family drama often occurs seconds or minutes after the fight. In the courtroom, emotions usually have subsided and memories have faded. The script is refined. The actors are polished and rehearsed. They are prepared to massage the facts to spin the case their way. They've had time to come up with convincing excuses and explanations. Accordingly, what transpires in the courtroom is not as reliable or truthful as the spontaneous eruption of the unrehearsed family drama.

Lawsuits Are About Persuasion with Credibility

Most juries begin a trial with a healthy degree of skepticism toward both sides. Moreover, in this day and age, juries seem to put little faith in the statements of lawyers. Jurors know that they may not get the whole, unvarnished truth and that each side is trying to sell them on a story. For this reason, you should focus on persuading the jury that it should believe your act in the play.

The key to persuasion is credibility. Credible means "worthy of belief." You have credibility when your audience concludes that you speak the truth, the whole truth, and nothing but the truth. If you and your act in the play are more credible than your opponent's, you will probably convince the jury that you should win.

Credibility is different from honesty. Credible means more than "truthful." For example, a three-year-old boy once told me that the moon is made of green cheese. He actually believed what he said and was telling what for him was the truth. However, his statement was not credible because it was obviously wrong.

You are credible not only if you appear to be telling the truth in good faith; you must also appear knowledgeable and informed. Your information must be reliable. You must know what you're talking about so that what you say can be accepted as gospel.

The "Truth" Depends on the Play

Because all actors and directors in the play are not equally credible, the theory that truth can be gleaned from the conflicting acts breaks down. At the risk of stating the obvious, a good lawyer is more persuasive than a bad lawyer. A good lawyer produces an organized, forceful, persuasive drama for the jury. A bad lawyer simply confuses everyone. A lawyer who appears warm, friendly, and honest causes a jury to like and identify with her and her client. A lawyer who is vague and confusing may remind jurors of the slick, traveling salesman hawking magic elixir door to door.

Mel Thomas opposed me in one of my first trials. He had to show the jury lots of letters written back and forth between the defendant and the plaintiff. He stacked them in a big, jumbled pile on a table in the courtroom. Because the letters were in no particular order, Mel spent much of the trial looking through the pile for the next letter. Afterwards, some of the jurors explained that Mel's client lost because Mel was so disorganized that the jury couldn't follow his presentation, didn't know if he showed them all of the important letters, and wasn't comfortable that he understood his case well enough to know what he was talking about. Mel did not present a credible "truth" to the jury.

Similarly, all witnesses are not equal. Most are ordinary people who reflect the entire range of education levels and personalities. Some are articulate, clear, sincere, trustworthy, honest, and convincing. Others cannot think or speak clearly. They give the appearance of lying even when telling the truth. Since all witnesses vary in their abilities to persuade a jury, the party with the best witnesses has a better chance of convincing the jury that his story is the truth.

Cathy Crabtree, a plaintiff I once represented, had an irritating habit of repeating the question asked by the defendant's attorney before answering. She made the lawyer repeat even a simple, innocuous question a couple of times. For example, the lawyer asked "Where is your checkbook?" Cathy responded, "Where is my checkbook?" The lawyer asked again, "Yes, where is your checkbook?" Cathy said, "You want to know where my checkbook is?" "Yes," the lawyer said, "where is your checkbook?" Cathy paused a few seconds, raised her eyebrows, gave a half smile, and said, "It's in my desk." Though she truthfully answered the question, she was evasive. The jury thought she was lying. Had she given a simple answer to a simple question, she would have been credible. Instead, she damaged her act in the play because she tried to outsmart the lawyer.

The "Truth" Depends on the Audience

In addition to the strengths and weaknesses of the actors and directors, the "truth" is, in part, determined by the attitudes of the audience. All jurors filter the evidence through their own values, experiences and predispositions. Jurors are rich and poor, black and white, young and old, Republican and Democrat. One juror may empathize more with the plaintiff and another with the defendant. They all have biases that affect their evaluation of witnesses, lawyers, and evidence. These attitudes impact each juror's conclusion about what is credible, fair, right, and wrong. Consequently, the "truth" for one juror can be vastly different from the "truth" for another.

Personality differences also affect each juror's understanding of the case. Jurors have different abilities and levels of intelligence. They see, hear, and perceive information in different ways. Some jurors perceive and remember more of what they see. Others are better able to process what they hear. Some are "morning people" who doze after lunch. Others don't get going until midafternoon. For these reasons, individual jurors remember different information presented in a trial. Moreover, two jurors rarely understand and remember the same information in the same way.

When you and a friend talk about a movie you have just seen together, you each may recall different scenes or lines or may remember the same scenes or lines in a different way. A scene that you think is hilarious may be boring to your friend. A scene you thought was fraught with meaning may have gone over or under your friend's head. A scene that offended you may have been funny to your friend. This lack of common recollection and understanding is exacerbated in a trial which may last two weeks rather than two hours and which jurors watch under duress rather than pay to see.

In addition to differences among individual jurors, the "truth" differs among juries as a whole because jurors communicate perceptions to one another with varying degrees of persuasiveness. As with any group, some jurors influence their peers more than others. Leaders and followers emerge. The final decision of right and wrong is driven by the conclusions of those jurors with the most credibility and influence over the group and their biases and perceptions.

The same bias and personality issues that affect individual jurors also influence the jury as a whole. Though each jury is a collection of individuals, as a group they may have personalities, abilities, and biases. One jury may be dominated by a collection of parsimonious, Yankee libertarians who believe that people should take care of themselves. Another may be a group of socialists who believe that the big company should always cover the "little guy's" expenses, regardless of right and wrong. Two juries watching the identical two-act play can reach different conclusions as to the "truth" and opposing decisions as to whom is right and whom is wrong. For these reasons, O. J. Simpson fought to have his criminal case tried in downtown Los Angeles, not the more affluent Santa Monica, so that he could get a more sympathetic jury.

I first learned about jury personality and its effect on the "truth" in the case of Myrtle Wilson. Myrtle was a farmer in North Carolina. On credit, she bought a combine she couldn't operate.

When her first payment came due, she decided she didn't want the combine and refused to pay. When the combine company sued, Myrtle claimed that she didn't have to pay because the machinery didn't work.

Myrtle was a great witness at trial. She was cute and spunky. When she was caught changing her testimony, she giggled politely and went on as if nothing happened.

We proved that the combine worked and that Myrtle had no defense. The only reason Myrtle didn't pay was that she didn't want to. The case should have been an "open-and-shut" win for the combine company. It was not.

A male juror seated in the front row fell head over heals in love with Myrtle. He was not, under any circumstances, going to allow the jury to enter any verdict for an out-of-state farm-equipment manufacturer against Myrtle. When the jury deliberated, the lawyers and clients waiting in the courtroom heard members of the jury screaming at each other and banging on the table.

The jury came back and rendered the verdict that Myrtle owed nothing to the combine company. The judge was shocked and ordered a new trial. Myrtle and the combine company eventually settled the case.

After the trial, we met some of the jurors in the parking lot behind the courthouse. They were extremely upset and apologized for the verdict. They told us that they knew that Myrtle owed the money and that the combine company should have won the case. They also said that they could not change the mind of the male juror who had fallen for Myrtle. They eventually felt compelled to capitulate and let Myrtle off the hook.

Myrtle Wilson's case is an anomaly. The jury usually does the right thing. However, jury personality and bias issues affect every case to some degree. Because the jury is the audience that counts, these issues are always critical in litigation.

The "Truth" Depends on the Judge

The abilities and biases of the judge also affect the case. Though judges may or may not ultimately decide who wins, they make rulings on issues of law and evidence that affect the outcome. Not all of their decisions are correct. Some may in part be based upon their opinions of right and wrong, which in turn may be based upon their values, experiences, and biases. Moreover, judges make comments or gestures which directly or indirectly, obviously or subtly, send messages to jurors about whom the judge thinks should win. A judge's body language is hard to hide. Though the jury decides the case, these ordinary citizens with no legal experience can be affected by a sense that the judge supports one side or the other.

I once defended a case in which the judge favored the plaintiff. Whenever the plaintiff's lawyer asked an objectionable question, the judge said in a calm, forgiving voice, "Well, I think I'll let it go this time." Whenever the plaintiff objected to a borderline question, the judge bellowed "OBJECTION SUSTAINED." Everyone in the courtroom, including the jury, knew that the judge wanted the plaintiff to win.

The Truth Depends on the Resources of the Parties

In addition to the personal characteristics and biases of the actors, directors, and audience, the financial resources the parties commit to their productions have a substantial impact on litigation. As with any other play, a well-financed production is often better than a show operating on a shoestring budget. For example, O. J. Simpson's highpriced, high-tech defense was much more effective than a single public defender with nothing more than a pen and notepad at his disposal would have been. O. J. might have been found guilty with a one-man, low-budget defense. Money affects a party's ability to hire good lawyers and the trial team's ability to develop and organize a case and present it in an effective and persuasive way.

> "Of course there's a different law for the rich and the poor; otherwise, who would go into business?
>
> —E. Ralph Stewart

Lawsuits Can Be Unpredictable

Due to all of these variables, trial results can be surprising. Guessing the jury's verdict is like picking the winner of a football game. Probabilities are assigned to different results, and odds are developed. However, because of the variables, no one can confidently predict the result in advance of the verdict.

Jury decisions can be plotted on a bell curve. After both acts of a play have been presented, and depending on how close the case is, you can often predict a likely result or range of results that can be plotted in the large part of a bell. However, since anything can happen, room must be left at either end of the curve for the unexpected. Moreover, sometimes cases have so many emotional, factual, and credibility issues that their outcomes cannot be predicted with any certainty. These cases are just a roll of the dice.

The best example of the unpredictability of jury verdicts is the O. J. Simpson criminal case. Everyone in the country knew the same facts about the trial from the extensive media coverage. Notwithstanding this identical universe of information, some pundits assumed a guilty verdict while others predicted "not guilty." All based their conclusions on different factors. Where they considered the same factors, they assigned different weights to them. No one was truly confident in the outcome until the jury rendered the decision.

The Jury's Truth Drives Lawsuits from the Outset

Notwithstanding the inherent unpredictability of jury verdicts, the parties' predictions of the jury's "truth" are critical issues in litigation from beginning to end. A plaintiff files a lawsuit because he believes that a jury will perceive a "truth" that will result in an award to him. A defendant refuses to settle early on for similar reasons. As the parties learn more about the case as it proceeds to trial, they constantly reevaluate their predictions of the jury verdict. These predicted outcomes govern the amount of time and money they commit to the lawsuit, whether and when to settle and, if so, at what price. Litigants should evaluate each option in light of the other alternative, the jury's decision. Everything that happens in litigation is good or bad only in relation to a prediction of the "truth" that the jury will embrace.

TO SUE OR NOT TO SUE, THAT IS THE QUESTION

2

I was at my son's soccer game one day when his coach and the referee started yelling at each other over a missed offsides call. The volume increased as coach and referee stood face to face, much like an umpire and manager at home plate. Suddenly, the referee backed away from the coach yelling at the top of his lungs, "Get away from me or I'll sue you. This is physical assault. I'll sue you." The coach had not touched the referee. The argument was no different from those at sporting events every day across America. Unlike most of these arguments, however, the referee threatened to resolve the dispute in court.

Lawsuits Have Limitations

Lawsuits are not designed to resolve every dispute in life. Though this may seem hard to believe in a world where children sue their parents for allowing them to watch too much television, the law doesn't protect against every harm or right every wrong. The law does not prohibit many types of conduct we may consider immoral, unethical, or offensive. For example, you have no claim against a store clerk who insults you with four-letter words when you return a defective toaster for the third time. Although offensive, it's a free country and that store clerk has a right to be as rude as he wants. Your remedy is never to set foot in the store again, not to go to court.

> "As a people we must somehow get over the notion that the solution to every problem is a lawsuit."
>
> —Ernest Conine

Similarly, if you share a new business idea with a potential employer without protecting it as a trade secret and the employer uses your plan but does not hire you, you may not have a claim. Though "stealing" your plan may be immoral or unethical, it probably isn't grounds for a lawsuit.

Many social issues such as gambling, drugs, euthanasia, and abortion highlight the differences between illegal conduct on the one hand and immoral or unethical conduct on the other. In some states, they may be considered immoral but not illegal, in others neither, and in others both. Though some argue that violence on television damages our children and leads to violence in America, the law does not allow you to sue a network because your children have been injured by watching too much bad TV. Similarly, a man who sat next to me on a plane said he wanted to sue the manufacturer of his favorite Scotch whisky because he drank too much and it made him a "stiff." The law as it stands today does not allow this type of claim.

Additionally, regardless of the validity of your legal claim, lawsuits are usually not worthwhile unless there is a significant injury. Lawsuits usually right wrongs through economic compensation in the form of an order that one side pay the other a specific sum of money. Consequently, and with certain exceptions, unless a plaintiff can show that the defendant caused a specific economic loss, she won't get much out of her lawsuit, even if she has an overwhelming legal claim. For example, you won't get much compensation from a defendant who accidentally fires a gun at you if the bullet barely grazes your bulky parka. Though the defendant may have been negligent in firing the gun, the fact that you weren't physically hurt means that you don't have much of an injury and won't recover any money. Similarly, if a stockbroker lies to you about a stock you buy, but the price of the stock goes up, you may have a great legal claim for fraud, but you don't have much of a lawsuit because you have no loss. Plaintiffs and their lawyers often ignore the fact that even if they're right on the law, a lawsuit without a big loss makes little sense. Rarely is litigation worth the fight when the monetary victory is insignificant.

> "It's like seeing your mother-in-law drive over a cliff in your new Cadillac."
>
> —Don Barrett, (describing his reaction when the jury found for his client but awarded no damages)

Focus on the Goals of a Lawsuit

The first step in deciding whether to sue is to figure out what you can get out of the case. Why do you want to bring the suit? What do you want at the end of the day? Are you angry? Is the lawsuit your revenge? Do you want to make your adversary suffer for offending you? Angry people like the soccer referee exclaim, "I'll sue the bum," without recognizing that emotional goals are rarely, if ever, achieved in litigation. Money doesn't always provide emotional satisfaction. Since most lawsuits are equally time-consuming and expensive for both sides, if you are suing solely for emotional reasons, you may suffer as much or more trauma in the litigation as your opponent and should probably not sue.

In a similar vein, many bring lawsuits when, deep down in their hearts, they just want the defendant to say he's sorry. An apology is not one of the remedies to achieve in litigation. If anything, a lawsuit will cause your opponent to become more defensive, entrenched, and indignant. In fact, filing a lawsuit is probably one of the best ways to ensure that you will not get an apology. Instead, you may want to call your adversary, explain why you are offended and see what he says.

> "In the strange heat all litigation brings to bear on things, the very process of litigation fosters the most profound misunderstandings in the world."
>
> —Renata Adler

For these reasons, you need to evaluate litigation solely in economic terms, however broadly defined. Without an economic analysis of the goals you can achieve, a lawsuit can be a waste of time and money.

Litigation is a lousy investment in most cases, but still some plaintiffs hope that they will "ring the bell" by convincing the jury to give them big bucks. They expect that they will have one of those cases reported in the newspapers where a plaintiff wins millions of dollars because of a scratch on a new car or a burn from hot coffee. These cases are very few and far between. In the vast majority of cases, because of the time necessary to get to trial, the cost of litigation and the fact that plaintiffs rarely recover as much as they want, litigation in and of itself is not good for the pocketbook. Lawsuits are about compensation for past losses, not making windfall profits.

Lawsuits are about more than monetary awards, however. Many legal wrongs are fixed through remedies other than cash payments. For example, three children of a wealthy landowner built a minibike race course on the back of their father's property.

They and their friends raced minibikes seven days a week, from dawn to dusk. Thereafter, they put lights on the course and rode their bikes well into the night. Because the children were an absolute nuisance, all of the neighbors filed a lawsuit in which they asked the court for an injunction to limit the hours the children could ride.

Land use and environmental cases often seek remedies that are unrelated to the payment of money. In these cases, courts enforce restrictions as to the size of residential building lots, the distance a home addition must be from the street or a septic system must be from an adjoining neighbor's well, whether a house can be built in wetlands, whether a mall can be built near a school or in a residential neighborhood, whether a factory can pollute the air, and many other regulations which affect the right to use land in a way that affects others.

Lawsuits may also be brought to enforce social policies concerning abortion, religious, racial, ethnic and free-speech rights. For example, many lawsuits have been filed to desegregate schools, change voting districts, and protect sensitive or controversial information.

Disputes are also litigated when the goals do not relate to the particular case. For example, a small lawsuit may be pursued to establish an important legal principle that will apply to a large number of similar cases. In these circumstances, a defendant may refuse to settle for far less than the cost of litigation because the judge appears to be supporting its case, the plaintiff is particularly unsympathetic, the facts favor the defendant more than the facts in similar cases, or the demographics of the pool of potential jurors suggest that the jury may be better for the plaintiff than in other cases. Any number of factors can turn an otherwise insignificant case into an important "test" case.

> "A lawsuit is a fruit tree planted in a lawyer's garden."
>
> —Italian proverb

Lawsuits may also be used to "send a message" to an adversary and others. For example, a large corporation may fight lawsuits with employees or competitors to demonstrate that it will be aggressive in asserting its business interests. The act of litigation proves that the corporation will not be pushed around.

Additionally, litigation, and business litigation in particular, can be used as a competitive weapon. Legal fees are often significant. Moreover, key employees may be pulled away from their day-to-day responsibilities to devote substantial amounts of time to assembling facts, being deposed, and managing the lawsuit. The cost in employee time and legal fees can be a drain on a business and cut into profits. Consequently, the relative value of entangling a competitor in hardball, "scorched-earth" litigation may motivate a lawsuit.

Finally, litigation may be pursued to delay payment of an obligation. If a lawsuit takes three years to go to trial, some defendants would rather wait to pay until the case ends, even though they will have to spend legal fees in the meantime. In deciding when to resolve a dispute and how much to pay, many sophisticated businesses balance the projected cost of defending the case for many years against the interest they would earn on the money they would pay to settle. The economic value of this delay convinces some litigants to settle "on the courthouse steps," right before the trial starts and legal fees begin to mount quickly.

> "The wheels of justice . . . they're square wheels."
>
> —Barbara Corcoran

Should You Sue?

In the context of these various motivations for litigation, anyone contemplating litigation should consider the following questions:

How Have You Been Harmed?

Have you been physically injured? Has your house, car, or other property been damaged? Have you lost money? Has a supplier reneged on a contract? Has a competitor stolen a trade secret? What, specifically, has happened to you that causes you to believe that you have been injured?

Who Hurt You?

In many cases, the answer to this question is easy. If another driver smashes into your car, or if a customer doesn't pay a bill, you know

Presuit Checklist

- ☐ How have you been hurt?
- ☐ Who hurt you?
- ☐ Do you have a legal claim?
- ☐ How good is that claim?
- ☐ What will you get if you win?
- ☐ Will you be satisfied with what you get?
- ☐ Can the defendant pay?
- ☐ How much money will the lawsuit cost?
- ☐ How much time will it cost?
- ☐ How much energy will it cost?
- ☐ How much emotion will it cost?
- ☐ What is your downside?
- ☐ Are you being objective?
- ☐ Are there better alternatives?

the answer. If, however, you have been treated by many different doctors, or taken many different drugs, or become sick from pollutants seeping into your drinking water, the issue may not be so clear. Before you file a lawsuit, determine who is to blame.

Do You Have a Legal Claim?

Even though you may have been harmed and have identified the person who harmed you, you may not have a case. If you buy stock that turns out to be worthless, you probably don't have a claim against the seller unless he gave you false or misleading information. The law does not ensure against all losses. Similarly, a lawsuit will not stop a taxi driver from insulting you or prohibit your neighbor from painting his house an offensive, florescent purple and parking his car on his front lawn, even though it reduces the value of your house by 20 percent. The law does not protect against all evils.

Certain technical legal rules can also preclude you from pursuing an otherwise valid claim. For example, if the facts which give rise to your claim occurred many years ago, your claim may be barred by a statute of limitations which prevents you from bringing a stale claim. Similarly, the statute of frauds prohibits claims based on certain contracts which are not in writing. For these reasons, determine at the outset whether you have a valid legal claim, or whether your case will be quickly thrown out of court.

How Good Is Your Claim?

There is no such thing as a sure winner. Since you never know how persuasive a witness will be until after he testifies or how well your lawyer will argue until she's done, and you never know in advance what a judge or jury will decide, there is uncertainty in every case. Because there are factual disputes in almost every case, and because you can't fully anticipate your opponent's production of the play, you should probably assume that you have at least a 20 percent chance of losing the case. Sometimes you have only a 20 percent chance of winning. Before starting a lawsuit, evaluate the strengths and especially the weaknesses of your case (and there are always weaknesses), and your opponent's strengths and weaknesses (there are always strengths), to determine your chances of success. Since you can lose any case no matter how good it looks, the issue is not whether there is a risk of losing, but rather, how much.

In evaluating your risk, keep in mind that one of the few certainties in litigation is that your adversary will tell a very different story from yours. For this reason, put yourself in your opponent's shoes to figure out what he would say in response to your claims. As you do this, remember the principle of selective perception—the tendency to emphasize the positive and filter out the negative. If you highlight your positives and downplay your negatives, you may not properly evaluate your strengths and weaknesses. Be balanced in your analysis. Then, determine a reasonable chance of losing assuming that the jury focuses on your weaknesses and your adversary's strengths. If you don't assume a reasonable probability of winning and losing every case, you may set yourself up for disappointment.

If You Win, What Will You Get?

Anytime you think about filing a lawsuit, consider what the court system can give you if you win. Can you win money? Will it be a nominal amount or enough to make the case worthwhile? Can the court make the children stop riding their minibikes in the middle of the night? As discussed more fully in Chapter 3, your remedies may be different based on the unique circumstances of each case. Evaluate your potential remedies before you start a lawsuit.

Will the Jury Give You Everything You Request?

More times than not, juries give plaintiffs less than they want and make defendants pay more than they think they should. Juries tend to believe that there is at least some truth in each act of the play. They often conclude that each side is partly responsible because "it takes two to tango." For this reason, you should probably assume that a jury will give you somewhat less than you think you should get. Moreover, depending on the nature of your claims, you will probably not recover your attorneys' fees or the other out-of-pocket costs you may have to pay. Consequently, in projecting the results of the case, focus not only on whether you will win or lose altogether, but also on how much money will be in your pocket at the end of the suit.

Can the Defendant Pay?

If you conclude that there is a reasonable possibility that you will obtain the remedy you seek, consider whether the defendant can meet her obligations. The key question is whether the defendant has the money to pay your damages or comply with a court order to fix your problem. In many cases, plaintiffs get "paper" judgments from defendants who don't have the money to pay. Nothing is more frustrating than to spend years litigating to win a million-dollar judgment, only to have the defendant file for bankruptcy and pay nothing. If that happens, the lawsuit has been a complete waste of time. Accordingly, before you start a lawsuit, ensure that the defendant can pay if you win. You may want to investigate her credit history or financial condition. You may also want to determine whether insurance or someone else is available to pay the amount you hope to recover.

Will You Be Satisfied with What You Get?

> "Litigation takes the place of sex at middle age."
>
> —Gore Vidal

Money can't buy happiness. Similarly, it cannot repair a reputation or replace a lost loved one. It is rarely the best revenge, which itself is often unsatisfying. Since the remedies available in lawsuits are generally oriented toward compensation for economic loss and little else, before starting a lawsuit, consider whether a complete victory on all fronts will satisfy your goals.

Are You Being Objective?

More times than not, lawsuits are filed when angry plaintiffs were mistreated or ignored. The doctor who refuses to return phone calls, the manufacturer who refuses to respond to repeated complaints about a defective car, or the collection agency that repeatedly sends threatening dunning letters long after the bill was paid are prime targets for lawsuits; however, three years later when the case is about to go to trial, the plaintiff's anger may have subsided and the emotional motivation for the lawsuit may no longer exist. Many plaintiffs in these cases wonder how they got into the lawsuit in the first place. Had they analyzed the case objectively at the beginning, they probably would not have filed the case. Though it may be hard to take the emotion out of your analysis, put yourself in the shoes of some anonymous juror who cares little about you, your case, or your emotions and resents having to leave his busy life to listen to your problems. Consider whether he would believe that you have suffered a significant harm. If some person who has no knowledge or personal interest in you would give you what you want, then a lawsuit may make sense. If that person would think you are making a mountain out of a molehill, then it's probably not worth the trouble.

> "Litigation should be a last resort, not a knee-jerk reflex."
>
> —Irving S. Shapiro

> "A lean compromise is better than a fat lawsuit."
>
> —English proverb

How Much Will It Cost?

Litigation can be very expensive in terms of time, money, and energy. You don't simply file a lawsuit and wait a couple of years to collect your money. You must spend a lot of time assembling information that supports your case, giving information to the other side through depositions and other discovery, getting ready for trial, and sitting through the trial. Depending on the financial arrangement with your lawyer for fees and the many expenses that arise in a case, a lawsuit will cost you at least some out-of-pocket money and perhaps a lot more. However, perhaps the greatest cost is your energy.

Lawsuits are often overwhelming. Almost every party to a lawsuit, except perhaps the litigation manager whose job depends upon the existence of lots of litigation, dwells at least some of the time on the case. You may dream about winning. You may toss and turn at night worrying about losing. Since the job of your opponent is to make you look bad and since no one is perfect, you may be concerned that someone will say something that will embarrass you in front of friends and family or make you look bad in front of your boss. Everyone worries about whether the jury will understand them, like them, and treat them fairly. Unless you have a strong claim, you may not want to devote what may be consuming energy to your case.

> "The ideal client is the very wealthy man in very great trouble."
>
> —John Sterling

What Is Your Downside?

In addition to losing the case, or winning less than you think you should, there are other downsides to litigation. For example, a lawsuit can generate publicity which may be good or bad for your standing in your community. Lawsuits can affect the way your friends, neighbors, co-workers, bosses, employees, or church members view you. For example, John Doe was recently approached by a group of families to join a lawsuit to block an elementary school redistricting plan, which they claimed discriminated in favor of minorities. Mr. Doe refused to join because he did not want his name associated with the case, regardless of its merits. He was not willing to risk the negative publicity in his home town.

Another big downside is the risk that the defendant will file a counterclaim against you. In sports, some say that the best defense is a good offense. For similar reasons, a defendant who is sued may sue the plaintiff back. Once this happens, you may

Alternative Dispute Resolution (ADR)

Alternative dispute resolution, and in particular mediation, can be an excellent alternative to litigation. As more fully discussed in Chapter 19, many turn to mediation because it has the following benefits compared to litigation:

- ◆ It's faster.
- ◆ It's cheaper.
- ◆ It's non-binding.
- ◆ It increases the role of clients.
- ◆ It reduces the role of lawyers.
- ◆ It leads to an agreement.
- ◆ It leads to a broad range of solutions.
- ◆ It may improve relationships.
- ◆ It usually works.

have a tiger by the tail because even if you drop your suit, the defendant can continue the countersuit against you. Accordingly, before launching litigation, think about whether you'll be sued back and whether you're willing to run the risk of being a defendant throughout the life of the lawsuit.

Are There Any Better, Less Burdensome Alternatives?

After you've run through the preceding questions, ask whether there are any better alternatives to litigation. For example, if you have some economic loss, but all you really want is for your adversary to acknowledge that she mistreated you, give her a call, tell her how you feel, and see how she responds. Under a cost-benefit analysis, a phone call may be a much wiser choice than a lawsuit that may take years to resolve. Ask whether there is any opportunity for a negotiated resolution. Consider alternative dispute resolution. Regardless of whether formal

> "Never stir up litigation. A worse man can scarcely be found than one who does this."
>
> —Abraham Lincoln

alternative dispute resolution is appropriate before litigation, there may be many alternatives that can give you more bang for your buck.

What Do You Do Next?

After you consider these questions and the remedies discussed in the next chapter, if you still want to file a lawsuit, it's probably time to talk to a lawyer.

Legal Remedies 3

Margaret Dalton lived on steep, winding Mountain Terrace. Tom Dixon lived next door on the uphill side. An old, leaking septic system was buried in Tom's front yard. Waste from the system constantly seeped down the hill onto Margaret's property. Tom was trying to sell his house, so he didn't want to spend the money to fix the system. He was hoping to stick the new owner with the responsibility. However, he was creating a serious problem for Margaret. Not only did she have an awful smell in her yard, but the seepage damaged her lawn and shrubs. Moreover, she was required to pay to clean up sewage from her yard every couple of weeks. Despite repeated requests, Tom did nothing to stop the flow. Finally, enough was enough and Margaret filed a lawsuit to get the court to force Tom fix the septic system.

Prior to filing suit, Margaret had to decide what she wanted from the court. First and foremost, she wanted Tom to fix the problem. Since a cash payment, however large, would not stop the seepage, Margaret needed a court injunction to force Tom to repair the septic system. Moreover, she was outraged at the fact that she had to pay to clean Tom's mess off her yard. Therefore, she also wanted a cash award to reimburse her for her cleanup costs. Finally, she wanted to recover the income she lost on the many days she had to stay home to supervise the cleanup and could not work, selling electrical equipment on commission. Consequently, Margaret had to consider many potential remedies that might be available from her lawsuit.

A remedy is what you win in a lawsuit. In most cases, it is limited to a monetary award called money damages; however, as in Margaret's case, when money damages are not enough to solve your problem, you can also get an injunction order from the court that requires the defendant to do or not do something.

Notwithstanding their importance, remedies are often ignored by lawyers and clients who focus too much on right and wrong and not on the results that can be achieved. Because the remedies available for your type of claim specifically determine what you will get at the end of the day, in order to avoid a hollow, moral victory, examine the remedies you want and that are available before you sue.

Since each claim is different, you should examine the available remedies in the context of the law and facts applicable to your case. However, basic issues relating to remedies are discussed below.

Money Damages

The amount of money damages you can recover depends upon many factors, including the type of claim, the nature and severity of your injury, the kinds of damages you have, and the certainty of your damages. Though damages are unique to each case, overriding issues include the following:

Damages Depend on the Nature of the Claim

The two general categories of claims that affect the measure of damages are contract and tort claims. A contract claim arises out of an agreement by you and the defendant to do something. If the defendant does not do what he promises, then you have a claim against him for breach of contract.

Damages for a breach of contract are measured by the difference between what you got and what you would have received if the defendant performed under the contract. You should recover the "benefit of the bargain"—what you would have received if the defendant did what he promised. For example, if the defendant promised to sell you a television for $500 but reneged on the deal, and you bought the same television from someone else for $550, then your damages would be $50—the amount the defendant's breach of contract cost you.

When your lawsuit is based on a tort, your damages may be different. A tort occurs when a defendant wrongfully injures you. The claim arises out of the defendant's wrongful act, not out of the breach of any contract or agreement. For example, if the defendant sells you a television that he represents as having stereo speakers and 500 channels, but it in fact has only one speaker and 13 channels, then you may have a claim in tort for fraudulent misrepresentation of the capabilities of the television.

When your claim is in tort, damages do not give you the benefit of your bargain because there was no bargain. Rather, they are intended to put you in the position you would have been in had you not been injured. Tort damages look backward to where you would have been if the injury never occurred, not forward to where you would be if the contract had been performed. In the television example, if you paid $500 for a television that was worth only $200, then your damages would be the difference between the amount you paid ($500) and the value of what you got ($200), or $300. Similarly, when a defendant negligently smashes your car, damages would be the amount necessary to fix the car. From an economic standpoint, damages should resolve the situation as if your car were never smashed.

In some cases, you can bring an action for both breach of contract and tort. This occurs, for example, when the defendant breaches the contract and makes false representations to you in the contract negotiations. Though often the same, the damages can be different. Consequently, analyze your potential damages in the context of your types of claims.

General and Special Damages

In evaluating your potential damages, consider the differences between general and special damages. General damages usually result from the wrongful acts committed by the defendant. For example, the cost of repairing Margaret's yard would be general damages in that sewage leaking from a neighbor's yard typically causes that type of loss. Similarly, the cost of repairing a smashed car would be general damages in that smashed cars usually need to be repaired.

Special damages, on the other hand, do not customarily flow from the injury but are peculiar to your circumstances. In Margaret's case, lost income from not working during the yard cleanup would be special damages in that lost income is not a customary result of septic overflow; rather, lost income damages arise from Margaret's unique circumstance of not working during the cleanup.

The distinction between general and special damages is significant in that special damages must be reasonably foreseeable. Foreseeable damages, though not customary, at the very least either happen in the ordinary course of events or are those which the defendant had reason to know about. For example, if Margaret won the state lottery but could not collect her winnings because she had to stay home and clean up seepage, she could probably not recover this loss from Tom. Unlike her lost income, damages for this unusual, unexpected injury would not be sufficiently foreseeable.

Additionally, special damages must be alleged separately in the complaint. If you don't plead your special damages, you may not be able to win them at trial, regardless of your evidence. Consequently, identify the special damages you seek before you file your complaint.

Damages Must Be Reasonably Certain

In order to recover general or special damages, you must prove them with reasonable certainty. You cannot get damages with vague, unsubstantiated requests for money. When your losses are economic, you must establish that you have lost the amount you claim you have. For example, to prove the cost of cleaning up her yard, Margaret would probably introduce into evidence bills from the cleanup company and cancelled checks used to pay those bills.

Damages for Margaret's lost income would be less certain and harder to establish. Unless she has evidence of sales she actually lost, or a clear track record of consistent sales per day that was disrupted by the cleanups, she may not be able to prove her damages with sufficient certainty. For this reason, and to the great frustration of many plaintiffs, businesses with no stable operating history have a difficult time recovering lost profits, even though they know they have lost money. A jury is not allowed to speculate about the amount of lost profits, and therefore can't award damages without proof of specific business losses, even though it's clear that there has been some economic injury.

Proof of noneconomic loss such as pain and suffering raises different issues. For example, how does the jury determine the amount necessary to compensate a man who loses his arm operating a defective printing press? Similarly, how does a jury estimate damages for a neck injury that will cause the plaintiff pain for the rest of her life? These damages cannot be proved with the specificity of out-of-pocket losses. Consequently, they are determined by more emotional arguments. For example, the man who lost his arm could claim that his arm is worth $500 per day, multiplied out over the rest of his projected life. Though not precise, arguments of this nature can lead to big verdicts.

Offsets to Damages

Some of my clients have stated that they don't want to minimize their injuries until after trial in order to keep their damages as high as possible. They say that they can fix the problem after the case is over. They want to ignore the rule that you must mitigate your damages as much as reasonably possible. Because of this duty, you cannot recover damages for losses you can reasonably avoid. For example, if Margaret could have saved her shrubs merely by watering them, but chose to let them to die to increase her damages so she could buy new ones, then she might not be able to recover these damages for failure to mitigate.

Further offsets occur if you receive a benefit. For example, if a construction worker with a permanent back injury gets a job as a computer programmer, wages earned from the new job would be offset against a claim for lost construction wages.

Damages Must Be Caused by the Defendant

You can only recover damages for injuries caused by the defendant. For example, Margaret could not funnel seepage to other parts of her yard in order to kill unwanted shrubs and seek to recover their value as part of her damages. Similarly, she could not use cleaning up her yard for a couple of hours in the morning as an excuse to take the entire day off and, at the same time, recover lost income from being away from work all day.

Calculation of Damages

The easiest way to calculate damages is to make a balance sheet. On the left side, list all of the economic gains flowing from the injury. For example, you should include wages you earn from the new job you were forced to take because of the injury. On the right side, list all of the losses. The amount by which your loss exceeds your gain is your damages. If the balance sheet is not weighted heavily to the loss side, it's probably not worth bringing your lawsuit.

Organizing Your Damages Before Suit

Because of the importance of damages, organize and analyze them as you evaluate your claim and prepare your complaint. Assemble all of your damages evidence, including bills, cancelled checks, and invoices. Tally them up to determine precisely how much you're owed. If you don't give them to your lawyer, save all documents that support your damages in a safe place. You will need them for discovery and the trial.

Notwithstanding the obvious value of this approach, many do not fully consider the amount of their damages and how they will prove them before filing a lawsuit. Consequently, discovery and trial preparation can be a mad scramble to assemble evidence. At the very least, this creates unnecessary tension and work. More important, in many cases, plaintiffs forego some of their damages because they can no longer find their evidence.

Punitive Damages

We've all read about multi-million-dollar punitive-damages awards for insignificant injuries; however, big punitive damages cases are few and far between. If you get them, consider them a windfall.

The standard for punitive damages in most cases is willful, wanton, or malicious conduct. In other words, the jury must find that the defendant is bad or incredibly reckless. As a practical matter, the jury must get angry at the defendant, which rarely occurs. Though you may think the defendant acted egregiously toward you, remember that the jury lacks your emotional involvement and is more willing to give the defendant the benefit of the doubt. Accordingly, in evaluating your chance to win punitive damages, assume that the jury will be much more moderate in its assessment of the defendant's conduct.

Attorneys' Fees

As a general rule, each side must pay its own attorneys' fees. Unless you are suing under a statute which specifically allows you to recover these fees, you will probably not get them. Consequently, even if you win damages that theoretically give you the

> ### Damages Checklist
>
> In order to ensure that a lawsuit is worth the trouble, consider the following:
>
> ☐ Do you have money damages?
>
> ☐ How much are they?
>
> ☐ Did the defendant cause the damages?
>
> ☐ Were the damages foreseeable?
>
> ☐ Are the damages certain?
>
> ☐ Can you prove the damages?
>
> ☐ Are there offsets to your damages?
>
> ☐ Can you win punitive damages?
>
> ☐ Can you win attorneys' fees?

benefit of your bargain or make you whole, you will ultimately receive less because you must pay legal fees.

Injunctions

An injunction is an equitable order by the court that the defendant do or not do something. Injunctions are appropriate only when monetary damages will not provide adequate relief. For example, in Margaret Dalton's case, all the money in the world could not make Tom Dixon's sewage stop flowing onto her yard. Only fixing the septic system could do the trick. For this reason, the court could grant an injunction to compel Tom to block the sewage flow.

T.R.O.s and Preliminary Injunctions

When your harm is irreparable and you can't wait through discovery and trial to get your relief, you may be able to get a temporary restraining order (T.R.O.) or preliminary injunction. These injunctions freeze the relationship and status of the parties until trial. For example, if a wholesale warehouse claims that its manufacturer is about to terminate its distribution agreement wrongfully, it may be able to get a T.R.O. or preliminary injunction to block the termination and continue the distribution arrangement at least through the trial. The distributor's harm could be irreparable in that once the manufacturer terminates, the relationship is over, employees could be fired, customers could be lost, and the distributorship could not be resurrected.

A plaintiff can get a T.R.O. without telling the defendant ahead of time. Applications for these *ex parte* (without notice to your opponent) orders are viewed skeptically by a judge because they don't give the defendant a chance to defend himself. They are granted primarily in cases in which time is short and the risk of injury is high. Moreover, in order to be fair to the defendant, they usually last no more than 10 days, which is typically long enough to schedule a full hearing on a preliminary injunction at which the defendant can appear and defend himself.

Unlike a T.R.O., preliminary injunctions may be in effect from their date of entry through the end of trial. Consequently, they can last through years of discovery. Because of their potential length, they are not entered without notifying the defendant ahead of time. Rather, the defendant can challenge the request for a preliminary injunction at a hearing at which the adversaries call witnesses and present documents and other evidence. Preliminary injunction hearings are much like minitrials and, in some cases, are even merged with an expedited final trial.

Temporary restraining orders and preliminary injunctions are not final decisions. They just preserve the *status quo* until the final decision. Since they are not final, you do not have to prove that you will ultimately prevail at trial. Rather, you need to show only that you have a likelihood of winning.

Because of this lower burden of proof, and because they are entered on an expedited basis after abbreviated discovery, T.R.O.s and injunctions are limited in scope. You will not get every remedy you seek in your lawsuit; rather, you get only that relief necessary to freeze the relationship until the trial. Tom Dixon, for example, might on a preliminary basis be ordered to block the sewage from flowing onto Margaret's yard but, after trial, be required to install an entirely new septic system which is a permanent solution to the problem.

Injunction Checklist

Before you start an injunction action, answer the following questions:

- ☐ Can you fix the problem?
- ☐ Can money compensate you?
- ☐ Is the problem continuing?
- ☐ Can the damage be undone?
- ☐ Will there be irreparable harm?

Prejudgment Remedies

In addition to temporary restraining orders and preliminary injunctions, garnishments and attachments may be available prejudgment remedies. These remedies allow you to collateralize the amount you hope to win at trial. For example, you might be able to get a security interest in the defendant's home or her bank accounts. You might also be able to take possession of property you claim the defendant wrongfully took from you.

For example, if Margaret was worried about Tom selling the house without fixing the septic system, she could attempt to attach the house. This attachment, much like a mortgage, would be a claim against the house for the amount of her monetary damages. If Tom didn't pay, Margaret could foreclose and sell the house to recover the amount of her judgment. Since an attachment would survive Tom's sale of the house, and the new owner would either have to pay Margaret if Tom didn't or lose the house, as a practical matter it would block Tom from selling his house without paying. Margaret could also ask the judge to order Tom's bank to freeze and hold the money in his account to pay her damages after the trial.

The rules for prejudgment remedies vary widely by state. They also contain many conditions and requirements. You should ask your lawyer about their availability before filing your lawsuit. Use them if you can. Tying up a defendant's assets before trial significantly increases your negotiating leverage in settlement discussions. Moreover, it ensures that money will be available to pay your judgment if you ultimately win.

Lawyer and Client in Partnership: What You and Your Lawyer Should Do for Each Other

Fred Lichtstein was the president of a regional auto-parts distributor. His biggest supplier was about to cut him off. Unless something happened, Fred would have to fire his employees and go out of business. Fred hired me to block the termination and recover substantial money damages. At our first meeting, he dumped an unorganized pile of documents on my conference room table and told me that he was a busy man with only 10 minutes to talk, and that if I was any good at all, I would get him everything he was owed in no time flat. Fred tried to pass all responsibility for the dispute from himself to me. He failed to understand that effective litigation is a partnership between lawyer and client, with each playing important roles.

In this partnership, lawyer and client have responsibilities and duties to each other. Though simple, they are often ignored as a lawsuit proceeds to conclusion. The failure to observe and fulfill these obligations causes conflicts between lawyer and client, and also reduces the chances of producing a persuasive play at trial.

What Your Lawyer Should Do for You

Your lawyer's duties to you are governed by the rules of professional conduct. These are ethical rules which each state adopts to regulate lawyer conduct. If lawyers fail to abide by these rules, they can be penalized and, in egregious cases, their license to practice law can be revoked. There are three core duties which are set out in the rules: competence, loyalty, and communication. Though these rules may seem simple on the surface, they can get complicated in their application.

Lawyer Competence

Under the rules of professional conduct, lawyers are competent if they have the necessary legal knowledge and skill and are sufficiently thorough and prepared to do a reasonably good job. Necessary legal knowledge and skill involve a balancing of many factors, including the complexity of your case, the lawyer's experience with your legal and factual issues, whether the lawyer can refer the case to or consult with a lawyer with more experience and competence, whether special problems might arise, whether there is an emergency, and how much is at stake. Just as a podiatrist shouldn't perform open heart surgery, a residential real estate lawyer shouldn't try an antitrust case. Necessary knowledge and skill are easily determined in some cases, however, since there is no clear definition, it is difficult to determine in other instances.

Sufficient thoroughness and preparation are equally vague. This standard also involves a balancing of factors, including the amount of time the lawyer can and does devote to your case, the size of the case, whether there is an emergency, and similar factors. If the lawyer doesn't begin to prepare the case until the day before trial or misses critical deadlines, he obviously hasn't fulfilled his duty. However, each lawsuit is different, and the standard is applied on a case-by-case basis.

Legal standards aside, to fulfill the duty of competence, a lawyer does not have to be great or even good; rather, a competent lawyer is not a bad lawyer. Though you have a right to expect excellent representation, your lawyer's failure to live up to your expectations does not mean that she is incompetent.

> "Don't try to instruct your lawyer. If you do, you've got the wrong lawyer."
>
> —John T. Nolan

The critical practical issue in evaluating whether your lawyer breached her duty of competence is whether her mistake harmed you. For example, if a judge dismisses your case because your lawyer ignored a court order, then you may have a claim against the lawyer for the amount you would have recovered from the defendant. In a malpractice case, you need to show that you lost money or were otherwise injured because your lawyer didn't do her job.

Regardless of your legal rights, you do not want to find yourself considering a malpractice claim. You should be able to find a good lawyer who will not put you at unnecessary risk. If you are concerned about your lawyer's competence, you may want to review your case with another lawyer and perhaps hire a new one.

Lawyer Loyalty and Conflicts of Interest

A lawyer has a duty of undivided loyalty to his client. In other words, your lawyer must do his best to promote your goals and interests. He should be prompt and diligent. He should do what you want, not what he wants.

When lawyer and client do not communicate well and a lawyer does not understand her client's objectives, she may pursue what she thinks are her client's goals instead of the actual goals. Moreover, some lawyers think they know what's best regardless of their client's stated objectives. To ensure that your lawyer is always attentive to your goals, periodically review them and how you will attain them together in your partnership.

> "I'd rather have my hand cut off than betray the interests of a client."
>
> —Raymond Burr as Perry Mason

An important aspect of the duty of undivided loyalty is the rule that a lawyer will have no conflict of interest. This rule provides that a lawyer cannot represent you and your adversary, even in different cases, unless you both consent. Any waiver of a conflict of interest must be voluntary after you have reviewed all important information that relates to the conflict.

Problems can arise when a client waives a conflict of interest without fully appreciating the extent of the conflict or the waiver. For example, a lawyer for Stamford Steel Company asked if he could sue the company on behalf of a customer who claimed that the steel he bought had microscopic flaws. When the lawyer said that the dispute was small, would be quickly resolved, and was no big deal, Stamford Steel waived the conflict and allowed the lawyer to sue. To the surprise of Stamford Steel, its customer asked for hundreds of thousands of dollars in money damages. Moreover, it had to produce thousands of pages of documents and its employees sat through a week of depositions in the discovery phase of the lawsuit. Stamford Steel had no idea that the case would be that difficult when it agreed to the waiver. Since it was not adequately informed, the company's waiver may not have been knowing and voluntary.

Every lawyer knows of situations where "no big deal" turns into a major lawsuit, the clients are at each others' throats, and both are mad at the lawyer who asked for the waiver. In the end, no one is happy. The only thing the adversaries agree on is that the lawyer shouldn't have asked for the waiver in the first place.

If a lawyer asks you to waive a conflict of interest, make sure you understand fully the specific conflict you're being asked to waive, as well as the potential practical and legal consequences of the waiver. Ask about the amount of the dispute and your potential damages, the specific nature of the claims, and the burden of document production, depositions, and other discovery. You may want to retain another lawyer to advise you as to whether you should waive the conflict. Remember that if both adverse clients do not waive the conflict, then the lawyer cannot represent either party in the dispute.

Even when no actual conflict exists, be cautious of the lawyer who hopes to represent your opponent in the future. There are many lawyers in this country. The competition for good clients is fierce. Your lawyer may have a chance to be hired by your adversary once your case is over and your opponent's next case comes along. Some lawyers keep this possibility in the back of their minds as they represent their clients.

Another type of conflict of interest is the positional conflict. It arises when the claims or defenses your lawyer should assert on your behalf are contrary to the interests of his other clients, even though those other clients are not involved in your case. For example, a lawyer who typically represents banks in collection actions may not be able to defend you in a collection suit brought by a bank because he might be required to assert defenses on your behalf that his other bank clients would object to. Similarly, lawyers who usually defend medical malpractice cases may not be able to represent you in a suit against your doctor.

Notwithstanding your lawyer's duty of loyalty to you, he is also a licensed professional and an officer of the court. Consequently, he has separate responsibilities to the legal profession, your opponent, the judge, and the court. His loyalty to you is limited by restrictions imposed on him by these other obligations. For example, regardless of your demands, he cannot make false statements to the judge, help you present false evidence, or assist you in criminal or fraudulent acts. He must also tell the judge about law that hurts your case. If you intend to violate these rules, your lawyer may not be able to represent you in the case.

Lawyers in many courts are also bound by Rule 11. This rule provides that every document filed with the court shall be signed by an attorney or, where a party is unrepresented, by the party. If not signed, the document is rejected. In signing, the lawyer implicitly represents that the document is not filed for any improper purpose such as harassing the opposition, that the contentions are not frivolous, that the facts alleged are supported by the evidence, and that the legal analysis is based on the law or a good-faith argument for extension of the law. In other words, the person who signs the document represents that he has researched the law and the facts and that the filing is proper. If a judge concludes that this rule has been violated, he can sanction the party and/or the lawyer. Sanctions can be severe. For example, the court can order that the opponent's legal fees be paid, assess monetary penalties, or even dismiss the case.

Your lawyer also has a duty to be fair to your opponent and her lawyer. For example, he cannot tamper with documents, obstruct your adversary's access to evidence, make frivolous objections, or, as a general rule, make life difficult for your adversary without good reason. When you tell your lawyer to be aggressive and not give an inch, he should take all reasonable steps to assert and protect your legal rights but do so in a professional manner. The bottom line is that your lawyer should do everything he can to represent your interests within the bounds of the ethical rules.

Your Lawyer Has the Duty to Communicate with You

A key to lawyer-client relations is communication. In order for your lawyer to do everything she can to help you achieve your goals, you and she must understand each other. If she doesn't comprehend your goals or how you want to achieve them, or if you don't know what your lawyer is doing, you have a problem. Your lawyer will be less able to help you, and this will reduce your chances of getting what you want.

The critical duty of communication has two aspects. First, your lawyer should inform you about the status of your case and promptly comply with your reasonable requests for information. She should also explain your case, its strengths and weaknesses, to the extent necessary to permit you to make informed decisions about how the case should be handled. Though apparently simple, these two rules are not always easy to apply.

> "About half the practice of a decent lawyer consists in telling would-be clients that they are damned fools and should stop."
>
> —Elihu Root

A lawyer's view of these duties may be very different from the client's. A lawyer usually is an expert in his field. The client often knows very little about the process. What is obvious for the lawyer may be complicated for the client. The client may complain that she is being ignored even though the lawyer believes that he has explained the issues over and over again. Lawyer and client working in partnership need to bridge this communication gap to ensure that they are on the same page at all times.

Aside from differences in knowledge and expertise, like friends and families, lawyers and clients have different conceptions of responsiveness. Some lawyers are terrible at returning phone calls. Despite repeated requests from clients, others seem incapable of providing copies of court filings and other documents. Conversely, some clients drive their lawyers crazy. They call frequently, even though they know the lawsuit will take years and nothing happens on a daily basis. Other clients seem to view their lawyers as their psychiatrists. For example, Cathy Crabtree called me constantly to talk not only about her case, but also about problems with her friends, children, and husband. Most of our conversations involved everything but the case. Because our phone calls were tedious, I tried to avoid talking with her as much as possible.

> "If you're a litigating attorney, always discuss tactics with the client at the trial. Not only will this surprise your adversary but your client as well."
>
> —Arthur Grebler

When we really needed to discuss her lawsuit, I was reluctant to call for fear that I would become bogged down in her personal life.

The bottom line is that lawyer and client must strike a balance. The lawyer must remember that the client is emotionally involved in the case and often needs to talk about it. The lawyer must also realize that communication gives the client confidence that he is paying attention to the case and will keep the client informed. The client, on the other hand, must remember that the lawyer has other cases and other things to do in life, and can rarely afford to devote full-time attention to one client or one case. A reasonable give and take between lawyer and client is the key to effective communication.

The second part of the communication rule—that the lawyer explain the case to the client to the extent necessary to permit the client to make informed decisions—has less room for give and take. If an important issue must be decided, the lawyer should call the client, explain the issues in detail, discuss the pluses and minuses, and give whatever other advice is necessary to assist the client in making the decision. If the lawyer doesn't provide sufficient information, and either makes the decision for the client or causes the client to make the decision without adequate information, then the lawyer has breached his duty of communication. If this occurs, the lawyer is in effect substituting her decision for her client's.

Notwithstanding this prohibition, some lawyers make decisions for their clients all the time. They may assume either that they know what the client wants or that there is no need to talk with the client who will agree with their advice anyway. This may be particularly true under a contingent-fee arrangement, in which the lawyer wants to keep his costs down and spending time with the client does not bring him economic benefit. Since you have the right to adequate information and to make your own decisions, be sure that your lawyer tells you all you need to know when you need to know it.

This does not mean that the lawyer can make no decisions. Though every decision is technically the client's, the lawyer needs some flexibility. Under a reasonable working relationship, the lawyer should be able to make many decisions on her own that do not affect the outcome of the lawsuit. For example, you may allow your lawyer to give your opponent an extra ten days to file a document without your prior consent. The extension is probably not significant to the case and would probably be granted by the court anyway. Moreover, the court would probably not appreciate your lack of cooperation if you opposed it. If you don't feel comfortable giving your lawyer the discretion to handle small matters on his own, perhaps you need a new lawyer.

To increase your willingness to communicate with your lawyer, as part of the duty of loyalty, your lawyer must keep confidential any information you give to him. Consequently, he cannot reveal information to your adversary or anybody else unless you authorize it in advance. The purpose of this rule is to enable you to tell your lawyer everything about the case—the good, the bad, and the ugly—in order that your lawyer can give you complete, thorough, reasoned advice and represent you to the full extent possible. The only exceptions to this rule are when the lawyer believes the client is about to commit a serious crime or in order to permit the lawyer to defend himself when sued by the client. Since these rules rarely come into play, the bottom line is that your lawyer should not tell anybody anything you tell him without your permission. Therefore, you should be able to tell your lawyer the whole story with confidence.

Notwithstanding these duties and protections, lawyer-client communication can be ineffective. For example, Dick Mercer took substantial amounts of money out of a company he ran and used these funds for vacations, lavish meals, automobiles, and other personal expenses. When the other directors of the company found out about it, they sued to get the money back. Dick had no defense. The jury was going to make him pay—the only question was how much. Time and again Dick's lawyer, Jeff Roberts, told Dick that he would lose. Dick repeatedly told Jeff that he was crazy. Dick was convinced he would win because he was trying to help the company, and the jury wouldn't care how much money he took. Dick went so far as to make Jeff write on a paper napkin that Dick was "definitely going to lose the case." Dick was going to make Jeff eat the napkin "when" Dick finally won. Needless to say, the case was a disaster. The jury decided that Dick had to pay back almost $1 million.

Dick could have settled the lawsuit before trial for under $100,000. Settlement was never a realistic option for Dick, however, partly because Jeff and he never really understood each other. Though Jeff repeatedly attempted to explain the issues to Dick so that he could evaluate the case, Dick never seemed to acknowledge Jeff's opinion of his risk of loss. Though Dick had the right to make his own decisions and to believe in his case, the

What Your Lawyer Should Do for You

- Know the law
- Know the facts
- Know how to try a case
- Prepare your case
- Work hard
- Represent only you
- Avoid clients like your opponent
- Respect your confidences
- Explain the process fully
- Explain your strengths and weaknesses
- Listen to you
- Answer your questions
- Follow your instructions
- Allow you to make important decisions
- Be a partner

lack of common understanding was not helpful to lawyer-client partnership. Because of the significance of communication, if you don't understand your lawyer and don't acknowledge that his opinions have at least some value, you may need a new lawyer.

What You Can Do for Your Lawyer

Since the lawyer-client relationship is a partnership, you have responsibilities to your lawyer. These duties are geared toward maximizing the ability of your lawyer to represent you to the best of her ability.

Tell and Give Your Lawyer Everything

The main thing you can do for your lawyer is to tell her the truth, the whole truth, and nothing but the truth. Tell her the complete story, from beginning to end. Don't leave out something you think is unimportant or unnecessary. Facts that seem irrelevant to you may be critical to your lawyer. Moreover, don't hesitate to reveal embarrassing or bad facts. Nothing frustrates a lawyer more than to be told a damaging fact halfway through a trial when it's too late to negate its impact.

You also want to immediately give your lawyer all of the documents you have that relate to your case. Diligently search everywhere to find every document that might possibly apply. Don't give your lawyer a few documents here and a few documents there as you happen to stumble upon them. Your lawyer needs all of the documents from the beginning in order to work with you to develop an effective strategy.

Marvin Harris seemed to be pulling documents out of his hat throughout our case. One month he'd find documents in his office. The next month in the attic, and then in a file storage area and at home. Then the cycle of office, attic, file storage, and home seemed to start over again. One day in the middle of the trial, Marvin showed up with a box of very important documents that our adversary had requested months before and that hurt our case significantly. The opponent's lawyer thought we were intentionally withholding documents. She was irate that she didn't have the documents before the trial. The judge was livid because he thought we were sandbagging the other side. I was angry because I should have seen the documents long before. Marvin's only explanation was that he didn't look hard enough to find them. This was no excuse. You need to look high and low for everything that may relate to the case and give it to your lawyer immediately.

Full, complete, early disclosure enables your lawyer to be your advocate. His job is to convince the audience that your story is true. His ability to persuade depends upon his own credibility. Developing credibility in this age of lawyer distrust can be difficult. Statements by lawyers are viewed with great skepticism by many jurors. Since the greater your lawyer's credibility, the better your chances of prevailing, enhancing your lawyer's credibility should be one of your goals.

Your lawyer's credibility is based in part upon what you tell him and the documents you give him. His information about the case comes largely from you, especially before he has learned about your opponent's position in discovery. If your lawyer thinks that he does not know all the facts, then he may be concerned about the reliability of the information he uses to argue your case. He may worry that contradictory information will come out that will cause the judge, the jury, or your opponent to believe that he isn't telling the truth or doesn't know the truth, either of which will diminish his credibility.

Concern over whether she has all of the facts may show in your lawyer's advocacy. She may not appear confident in your story. She may hedge her bets. In a worst-case scenario, your lawyer can be as concerned about protecting her credibility as she is about being your advocate. As one of my partners once said, "I have nothing to sell but my reputation." Preservation of this reputation is of paramount interest to lawyers. They won't risk it on clients.

As your lawyer evaluates your lawsuit, he will consider your credibility. Lawyers look for inconsistencies and missing facts throughout a case. Part of the job is to test not only your opponent's credibility, but yours as well. Only through this testing can your lawyer properly advise you as to the merits of your claim. A lawyer also does this in order to determine how much he can rely on what you tell him.

Cathy Crabtree was questioned extensively about the location of money she took from her company. Though no one had proof, the judge, our opponent, and I knew that she was hiding something. Cathy's credibility deteriorated to the point that I had to stop making arguments based on what she said. I did not trust the facts she told me, and the judge did not trust any arguments based on those facts. The only way our case retained any semblance of credibility was to ignore Cathy's testimony completely. Her case would have been much stronger if she had told me the damaging facts, and we could have structured our argument to rely on the portions of her testimony that helped us.

Since everything you say to your lawyer is confidential, there is no need to hold back. In litigation, most of the embarrassing facts and "dirty laundry" come out eventually. Since surprises can be very damaging at trial, tell your lawyer all of the bad facts at the outset so that she can develop a strategy to diminish their impact. If you don't tell your lawyer everything, she won't be a strong advocate for you. If you can't confide in your lawyer, you should get a new one.

Discuss Your Goals and How to Achieve Them

Explain to your lawyer exactly what you want and why. Be specific in describing your goals. Since your lawyer's job is to help you achieve these goals, if he does not know what you want and why you want it, he cannot give you advice as to the best way to get it.

You should also discuss very clearly the important strategies and tactics. Ask about the pluses and minuses of each step in the process. Should you file a motion to dismiss? Do you need an expert witness? Is a trip to London for a deposition worth the money? Some lawyers employ tactics out of habit. Other times they want to demonstrate activity. Since lawyers tend to be cautious, some want to take more depositions than necessary to eliminate every uncertainty before trial. Do a cost-benefit analysis. Every time you discuss a tactic with your lawyer, ask whether there is a better, cheaper way to do it. This dialogue will not only assist you in making sure that every step is designed to meet your goals, it will also help you better understand your lawsuit.

Listen to Your Lawyer

You hired your lawyer presumably because you value her opinion and think she can help you win your case. At the risk of stating the obvious, you should listen to her. Curiously, many clients don't. After getting their feet wet, some clients begin to think that they understand the litigation process better than their lawyer. They forget that a good lawyer is essential to even the most experienced client. If you feel that you know more about litigation than your lawyer, or you don't want to listen to her, you may need a new lawyer.

Understand Your Lawyer

Your lawyer will give you much advice over the life of the case. You should understand this advice. If you don't, ask for explanations until you do. Don't assume that you will figure it out as time goes on. Don't worry about asking stupid questions. Your relationship with your lawyer should be one of complete trust and confidence. You should be able to ask him anything, however ridiculous, and he should answer. If you are not "on the same page at all times," then you both have a problem.

Understand Your Lawyer's Role

Though the lawyer is important to you and your case, he is still nothing more than your legal advocate and advisor. His job is to help you navigate the legal system to assist you in reaching your legal objectives. He is not your father, psychiatrist, or priest. His job is not to help you work out your personal problems. His role is strictly legal.

Make Your Own Decisions

Since your lawyer is only a legal advocate and advisor, you have to make your own decisions. You have to decide when to fight, when to settle, and how much to spend along the way. The purpose of the lawyer's duty of communication is to ensure that you have the information necessary to make these decisions, not to allow you to pass the buck to your lawyer. It is and will always be your case.

Pay Your Bills

You hire your lawyer to represent you under a contractual arrangement. Under this contract you may have a responsibility to pay fees and/or expenses. Most lawyers work hard for their clients and expect to be paid. By paying your lawyer, your relationship with her will be much smoother. You will also get better service. Human nature suggests that if your lawyer has two clients, she will invariably work first for the client who pays her fees on time.

> "To compensate for minor irregularities in the earth's rotation, official international timekeepers add one second to this day. U.S. law firms adjust their bills."
>
> —Dave Barry

Don't Ignore Requirements and Deadlines

Litigation is governed by many procedural rules and court-imposed requirements. You must do many things within specific deadlines. For example, you will have to file documents in court, produce your records, and appear at depositions. Serious consequences flow from the failure to comply with these deadlines, including, in egregious circumstances, dismissal of your case. At the very least, ignoring the rules can reduce your credibility. If

What You Should Do for Your Lawyer

- Tell him ALL facts.

- Give him ALL documents.

- Hold back nothing, even if it's bad or embarrassing.

- Tell him exactly what you want and why.

- Listen to him.

- If you don't understand, ask.

- Make your own decisions.

- Pay attention to your case.

- Participate in your case.

- Pay your bills.

- Be a partner.

your lawyer says you have to do something by a certain time, you should do it.

Be a Partner

Since a lawsuit is a partnership between lawyer and client, act like a partner with your lawyer. You are both part of the same team. Work together. If you and your lawyer function well in relation to each other, many of these other duties may fall into place. Conversely, if you can't work together, you will have other problems and may want to find a new lawyer.

How to Hire and Fire a Lawyer

5

Steve Thompson, an in-house lawyer who works for an equipment manufacturer, retains a trial lawyer in a law firm to represent his company. This lawyer never returns phone calls in less than a week, rarely lets Steve review court documents before filing, and consults with Steve on only the most major issues. Though this lawyer exasperates Steve, he still uses him because he's great in court and because others in the company like him.

Picking a lawyer who is right for you is essential to your lawsuit. This does not mean that you need the most experienced, famous or best lawyer. You need a lawyer who understands where you are coming from and who will help you get where you want to go, when and how you want to get there. Just as there are enormous differences among personalities generally, there are vast differences among lawyer personalities. A lawyer who is good for one client may be bad for another; it is important to get the right fit.

> "The public needs the equivalent of Chevrolets as well as Cadillacs."
>
> —Learned Hand

Hire a Credible Lawyer

An essential requirement for any lawyer is that he be persuasive and credible with your opponent. This credibility creates risk for your adversary and gives you negotiating leverage. Conversely, if your adversary believes that your lawyer is a blowhard who can't get the job done, then he will assume that the jury will not adopt your position, and you will fail to pose a serious threat. Accordingly, you will have little negotiating leverage, and your adversary will have no incentive to settle the case for a reasonable amount.

For these same reasons, your lawyer should be credible with your opponent's lawyer. Your adversary's lawyer is a key to convincing your opponent of the strength of your case. She can advise, for example, that you will be an excellent witness at trial and can convince the jury to award you lots of money. She can explain the significant risk of loss. She can recommend that your opponent settle and for how much. If your lawyer convinces your adversary's lawyer that you are a credible threat, then you increase the value of your case.

Finally, your lawyer must be credible with the judge. Even in a jury case, the judge makes many significant decisions throughout the life of the case. For example, he rules whether you can review information in discovery which your adversary wants to keep from you. He decides the law the jury must apply to the evidence it hears at trial. He even determines whether he, not the jury, should decide who wins or loses the case, or whether he should overrule the jury's verdict by ordering a new trial.

Lawyer credibility with the judge is particularly important because of the many different legal and factual issues that come up in the hundreds of cases the judge handles at any one time. Because the judge has so many decisions to make in so many different cases, she must rely on the representations of lawyers. Any judge will tell you that credible lawyers are essential to a smoothly functioning system. If the judge can't trust what the lawyers say about the law, then the judge or his law clerks must look up the law themselves, which generates more work. For this reason, the judge wants to rely on your lawyer. If he is credible, then the judge will trust what he says and give him the benefit of the doubt. If he is not credible, then the judge will rely on the other side. The lawyer with the most credibility has the greatest success in front of the judge and the best chance of winning.

Hire an Experienced Lawyer

In addition to credibility, there are other minimum prerequisites for your lawyer. For example, you don't want to hire a lawyer who has never been in court to defend you in a lawsuit. There are many things about litigation that a lawyer cannot learn in law school or books. Notwithstanding the lawyer in John Grisham's *The Client*, only through experience can you comfortably produce a persuasive play in court. Only by doing it can you consistently formulate persuasive lines of questions. Only through trial and error can you develop a sense of the tactics that do and don't work.

As you consider the experience of lawyers, be mindful of a lawyer who proudly calls himself a "litigator" but hasn't been the lead lawyer in many trials. There are many lawyers today, particularly in large law firms in urban centers, who claim to be trial lawyers but have very little trial experience. They do lots of depositions, review thousands of documents, attend numerous hearings, and then settle their cases before trial. You don't want a litigator practicing new trial techniques on your case. If you're serious about your case, hire a lawyer who can try it if you have to. Moreover, since lawyers in a community know who does and doesn't have trial experience, an inexperienced "litigator" may not pose much of a threat to your opponent. Consequently, your adversary will not be afraid of you and will not pay top settlement dollar.

In addition to general trial experience, a lawyer with experience in the legal and factual issues in your case is important. For example, much of the knowledge and experience of a lawyer who has litigated fender-bender cases throughout his life is not transferrable to a complex securities fraud case. The law and facts are completely different. You probably want a lawyer with not only general litigation experience, but also with experience in the legal and factual issues in your case.

When the lawyer has experience with your kind of dispute, consider whether she typically represents your side. For example, lawyers who represent employees often do not represent employers. For business and positional conflict reasons, they stay on the employee side of the fence. Similarly, lawyers who usually represent banks are often reluctant to represent borrowers against banks. Moreover, even if the lawyer is willing to take a case adverse to the interests of most of her other clients, think about whether you want her. For example, a borrower may not want to hire a lawyer whose livelihood depends in large part on bank work; rather, it may be safer and smarter to hire a lawyer who is aligned with your business and legal interests and won't have an incentive to pull any punches.

You also probably don't want a lawyer who says he always wins. He's probably lying. There's also an old saying that a lawyer who always wins settles too easily. In other words, the lawyer tries only the cases he can't lose and settles everything else. If you have a lawyer with a reputation for being afraid to try the tough cases, then you will not generate risk for your opponent and will not maximize negotiating leverage for settlement discussions.

Hire a Lawyer with Whom You're Comfortable

You should hire a lawyer whose personality you can live with. At various times during the case, you will work very closely with her. You don't have to love her, but you should be able to tolerate her. Is she soft-spoken or loud? Can you speak your peace, or does she cut you off in mid-sentence? Does she value your opinion and treat you with sufficient respect? Does she have the appropriate "bedside manner"?

A personality conflict often arises over the difference between the lawyer who sees all of the options, however remote, and discusses them with the client *ad nauseam*, and the direct, to-the-point lawyer who, with little discussion, cuts to the chase. Some clients like to process every possible legal and factual issue, option, and outcome. Others want a short, succinct summary and recommendation. The long-winded lawyer drives the to-the-point clients crazy. The succinct lawyer makes the process-oriented clients feel ignored. You should probably find a lawyer who processes information and addresses issues the same way you do.

You also want a lawyer who is sufficiently responsive to you. Some lawyers return phone calls in five minutes, others in five days. Some clients want calls returned in five minutes. For those like Steve Thompson, five days is acceptable. Make sure that the lawyer you hire is sufficiently attentive. If not, he will frustrate you.

Interviewing a Prospective Lawyer

Interview a lawyer before hiring him. He should give you a free consultation to discuss your case generally and allow you to ask any questions you may have. As you talk with him, keep in mind your primary need for a lawyer who is credible and persuasive with your opponent, his lawyer, the judge, and the jury. All other factors should be viewed in the context of this overriding requirement. These other factors include the following:

How Does the Lawyer's Office Look?

Is it neat and professional? Are the staff members courteous when they greet you? Are they polite on the phone? Does the office appear to be a well-run, professional organization? Though not necessarily evidence of litigation experience, by and large, good lawyers have good offices. Practicing law without an effective organization behind you is difficult. Moreover, a lawyer with a professional office gives her and you credibility with your opponent. Through this professionalism, your lawyer communicates that she knows what she's doing. You communicate that you have hired a top-gun lawyer who must be reckoned with.

> "It is not unprofessional to give free legal advice, but advertising that the first visit will be free is a bit like a fox telling chickens he will not bite them until they cross the threshold of the hen house."
>
> —Warren Burger

What Is the Lawyer's Experience?

Does the lawyer have real trial experience? Has he handled cases with legal and factual issues similar to the issues in your case? Who did he represent? What were the results of these cases? Ask him to describe the similarities and differences between other cases and your case. Don't simply rely on his statement that he's "handled lots of these cases before." Since each case is different, question claims that other cases are "just like yours." Beware of the lawyer who claims to be an expert in everything that relates to your case. Except in specialized areas, new issues are likely to come up. Good lawyers have a healthy respect for what they don't know, and they admit it. If the lawyer is "blowing his horn" too much, he may not be for you.

> "The courtrooms of America all too often have Piper Cub advocates trying to handle the controls of a Boeing 747 litigation."
>
> —Warren Burger

Who Are the Lawyer's Other Clients?

Are the lawyer's other clients similar to you? For example, you don't want to take a small fender-bender case to a corporate litigator who represents only Fortune 500 companies. You will fall through the cracks. Also ensure that there are no positional conflicts and that the lawyer doesn't usually represent clients like your opponent. The bottom line is that you probably want to be a fairly typical client with a fairly typical case.

Does the Lawyer Have All the Answers?

In most cases, the law and facts must be researched which, depending upon the results, may have a substantial impact on your case. Most good lawyers will, after listening to your story, identify the issues that must be checked out before they can opine on the strengths and weaknesses of your case. They know that the law is dynamic. They also know that the facts develop as a case is investigated. Generally speaking, only lawyers who miss the issues, or intentionally ignore them to convince you to hire them, give a strong opinion on the spot.

Can You See a Writing Sample?

Though rarely done, ask for a sample document the lawyer wrote and filed in court. Many lawyers talk a good game. However, much of the important work in litigation is written. If a lawyer cannot draft a clear, well-organized, written argument, then she cannot effectively advocate your position to the judge. Good writing also enhances your lawyer's credibility with the judge and your adversary, thereby increasing your lawyer's persuasiveness and the value of your case. Moreover, if your lawyer cannot write well, then she may not be able to organize your case logically. Since clear, organized, logical arguments are essential for successful litigation, an inability to write well should concern you about whether the lawyer can effectively present your portion of the litigation play at trial.

> "Be prepared, be sharp, be careful, and use the king's English well. . . ."
>
> —Robert N.C. Nix

In addition to being well written, the sample should be neat, clean, and free from typographical errors. If the lawyer's written product does not look professional, then the judge and your opponent will not think she is professional. In actuality, appearance doesn't change the meaning of the words on a page. However, just as the same wine seems better in a crystal glass than in a paper cup, a neat, clean document is more persuasive than one with typos and misspelled words. You may also question whether a lawyer who does not give you a professional-looking writing sample cares about her work and will care about your case.

Who Will Actually Work on Your Case?

Oftentimes, particularly in a large law firm, you may hire one lawyer only to find that other lawyers work on your case. For example, you may hire a 55-year-old senior trial partner, but discover that 99.9 percent of the work is done by a second-year associate with little or no experience. Since lawyers have different levels of experience, can perform tasks with different levels of efficiency, and have different billing rates, you may want more than one lawyer to work on your case. For example, you may not want to pay a senior partner to spend days in the library doing legal research. Similarly, you may not want a first-year associate cutting his teeth on your case. The key is to get the right person with the right billing rate for the right job. However, lawyer and client don't always agree on who should do what. Consequently, lawyer staffing can be a big source of lawyer-client tensions. You should ask at the outset who will be doing what on your case and why. If the lawyer you interview indicates that someone else will be doing a substantial amount of work, interview that person as well. You need to know and be comfortable with the lawyer you will be dealing with on a day-to-day basis. You also need to ensure that lawyers with the appropriate level of experience are performing the many tasks in your lawsuit.

Is the Lawyer Experienced in ADR?

As discussed more fully in chapter 19, alternative dispute resolution (ADR) is in many cases an efficient, cost-effective, creative means of resolving disputes; however, not every lawyer has the knowledge, experience, and inclination to use it when appropriate. For example, the aggressive "hired-gun" trial lawyer may have no interest in ADR options, even though they may further your goals.

When you discuss ADR, press the lawyer for his specific ADR experience. A lot of lawyers "talk the ADR talk, but don't walk the ADR walk." Ask him about specific disputes he has mediated. Have him describe in detail the legal and factual

Lawyer Interview Checklist

When you interview a prospective lawyer, consider the following:

- ☐ What is the office like?
- ☐ What is the lawyer's trial experience?
- ☐ Does she have ADR experience?
- ☐ What is the lawyer's experience with cases like yours?
- ☐ Is she involved in professional organizations?
- ☐ Does she have all the answers?
- ☐ Does she have a healthy respect for the unknown?
- ☐ Is she articulate?
- ☐ Does she ask good questions?
- ☐ Is her writing sample organized and well written?
- ☐ Who will work on your case?
- ☐ How will tasks be divided?
- ☐ How do her other clients compare with you?
- ☐ Who are her references?
- ☐ What are the billing arrangements?
- ☐ Is she credible?
- ☐ Do you like her?
- ☐ Do you trust her judgment?

circumstances of these cases and the results achieved. If he isn't well versed in ADR and doesn't believe that it is a viable option in most cases, you should be concerned that he may be more interested in litigating cases and earning legal fees than in resolving your dispute in the most efficient, cost-effective manner at terms that are most beneficial to you.

Can You See the Lawyer's References?

Call the references to question them in detail about their cases and the lawyer's performance. Compare the facts and law of their cases to yours. Determine whether the lawyer understood their facts and the applicable law. Ask whether she was prepared for depositions and court. Did she ask clear questions and make persuasive arguments? Did she write well? Did she appear to have credibility with the judge? Did she keep her client informed? Was she responsive? Were the bills fair? Were there any problems? Analyze this information in relation to your dispute to determine how their experiences would apply to you.

Other Information About Lawyers

In addition to facts gathered in the interview process, other information can be helpful in selecting a lawyer. For example, there are readily available public sources of information about lawyers that are invaluable. These include the following:

The Martindale-Hubbell Directory of Lawyers

These volumes contain biographies of lawyers and law firms worldwide. In them you can discover where the lawyer went to college and law school, the year he graduated, the places where he is admitted to practice law, professional committees and organizations to which he belongs, articles he has published, any specialty or expertise he may have and similar kinds of information. Moreover, by looking at his firm's biography, you can learn the areas in which the firm as a whole specializes.

National, State, and Local Bar Associations

Many lawyers are members of their national, state, and local bar associations. These associations have committees of lawyers who practice in particular areas of law. You can determine through a bar association whether the lawyer claims to have expertise in your particular area.

Certified Specialists

In some states, lawyers can be certified as specialists. These certifications generally require the lawyer to pass a test and meet requirements that demonstrate a high level of knowledge, experience, and expertise; consequently, certified specialists should be able to do the job.

Legal Fees

In addition to selecting a lawyer with the right personality and qualifications, you should find a lawyer who will work under a fee arrangement that is right for you and your case. You and the lawyer should agree to this arrangement before she starts work. The two most traditional fee arrangements are hourly billing and contingency. Under an hourly billing arrangement, the lawyer bills you at a rate of a certain number of dollars per hour. You are obliged to pay the fee calculated based on this rate for as many hours as the lawyer works on your case.

> "In law, nothing is certain but the expense."
>
> —Samuel Butler

Contingent-fee arrangements are common in certain categories of plaintiffs' cases such as personal-injury litigation, where, for example, a plaintiff is injured in an automobile accident or by a dog bite. Under these fee structures, the lawyer receives little or no money up front or throughout the litigation, but gets a percentage of the amount collected from the defendant. If you lose, the lawyer doesn't get paid. Although many states have statutes limiting the percentages lawyers may be paid under these arrangements, the traditional fee is one-third of any recovery.

In recent years, both the hourly billing and contingency-fee arrangements have come under fire. Clients complain that hourly billing structures give lawyers an incentive to do more work than necessary in order to run up the bill. Moreover, they argue that even lawyers who do not run up the bill have no incentive to be as efficient as possible. Finally, they claim that fees can be difficult to control because it can be hard to extricate yourself from litigation that seems to go on and on.

Clients raise the opposite objection with contingent-fee structures. Under this billing arrangement, lawyers have an incentive to do as little work as possible in order to maximize the fee in relation to the amount of the work. Clients are concerned that lawyers do not do all that they should, or at least have an incentive not to work in order to get the most bang for the buck.

In response to these tensions, some clients prefer a number of different "alternative" billing structures. The purpose of alternative billing is to shift some of the risk of the unforeseen events and expenses that invariably arise in litigation away from the client and to the lawyer and yet, at the same time, ensure that the lawyer has sufficient incentive to work hard. The lawyer is the expert in litigation and presumably is best able to project what will happen, when it will happen, why it will happen, and how much it will cost. For this reason, many clients contend that the lawyer should bear some of the economic loss if expectations are not fulfilled. Because alternative billing structures shift some of this risk to the lawyer, many lawyers hate them, and many clients love them.

> "I can think of no other business where you are rewarded for inefficiency. No matter what you sell, the fewer hours of labor that go into the product, the more you make. With lawyers it's backwards—the more time you take, the more inefficient you are, the greater your profit."
>
> —Alan Liebowitz

For example, some alternative billing arrangements impose limits or caps on the total fees which can be charged under an hourly arrangement. The client pays fees calculated on an hourly basis but only up to a certain limit. Once the cap is reached, the client pays no more. This arrangement requires both the lawyer and the client to project and agree upon the maximum cost of the dispute at the outset. The lawyer has an incentive to be realistic so that he doesn't end up doing a lot of work for free. He can't give the client a lowball budget and then reap the benefits of his error. Moreover, this structure shifts much of the risk of unforeseen events to the lawyer.

Budget or task-based billing is also gaining popularity. Under this arrangement, the lawyer develops a detailed budget which includes all of the major events that are likely to occur in the lawsuit. The client pays a fixed dollar amount for each itemized unit of work as it is performed. The cost of each segment is agreed in advance. Additionally, the budget dictates to a large extent when and in what order events will occur and fees will be paid. Moreover, it forces the lawyer and client to focus in advance on precisely what should and should not happen in the litigation and why. Through the process of developing the budget, the client and the lawyer must discuss each step in the lawsuit. This exercise enables the client to evaluate whether each tactic is worth the effort and money. Through this careful planning and analysis, the client gains greater knowledge of and control over her lawsuit.

Even if you don't agree to a budget-based alternative billing structure and instead agree on a more traditional hourly fee arrangement, a detailed budget is important. It should specifically identify each step in the litigation and how much it will cost. You should closely monitor your fees in relation to the budget to ensure that costs do not get out of hand. You have the right to expect that your lawyer will adhere to this budget, and you should object if your costs vary substantially.

In doing this budget, focus on the expenses you may be responsible for in addition to legal fees. Your lawyer probably will expect to be reimbursed for her many out-of-pocket costs, including filing and service fees, deposition and transcript costs, and travel expenses. Moreover, although the trend is for law firms to absorb ancillary charges as a cost of doing business, many law firms still charge internal expenses back to the client, such as telephone, fax, and overnight-mail charges. If the case involves lots of documents, copying charges can eat you alive. Moreover, expert witnesses can be very expensive. By the time all is said and done, costs in addition to legal fees can be in the tens of thousands.

As you consider retaining a lawyer, devote substantial thought to the type of fee arrangement that may be best for you and your case. Since different fee arrangements create very different incentives, make sure that the incentives work for you, not for your lawyer. If your lawyer refuses without good reason to agree to an alternative billing structure with appropriate incentives, consider going somewhere else.

Retention Letters

Your fee arrangement with your lawyer should be in writing and signed by both of you. Don't be surprised if your lawyer makes you sign one. In some states, a lawyer must sign a contract with his client.

The fee contract should specifically describe the work that the lawyer is hired to perform. If he's representing you in only one case, it should identify that case. If he is handling many matters for you, they should all be listed.

The retention letter should identify who will be working on your file. Since you are probably hiring a particular lawyer and not a law firm generally, the contract should state that the lawyer you want is responsible for your case. If many lawyers are working on the case, the letter should list them as well. If billing is under an hourly rate structure, the agreement should include the rates of those who will represent you.

The letter should explicitly state the respective obligations of you and your lawyer under the fee arrangement. For example, it should describe the frequency of billing, be it monthly, quarterly, etc., and the information contained in each bill, including the identity of each person performing work, the billing rate, the amount billed for each unit of work, a detailed description of the work, and the time spent performing the work. The letter should also outline your obligations to the lawyer, such as payment within 30 days of receipt of the bill.

Check whether the retention letter has an alternative-dispute-resolution provision which requires mediation or arbitration of any dispute between you and your lawyer. As discussed in Chapter 19, ADR may be a better way to resolve these sorts of disputes. Many retention agreements contain ADR provisions because they are beneficial to both lawyer and client.

Finally, the letter should describe the terms under which your lawyer can withdraw from representing you. Generally speaking, retention letters provide that a lawyer can quit at any time. However, once your lawyer "appears" in court by advising the court that he represents you, the judge has approval over his withdrawal. The judge should ensure that your lawyer does not bail out of your case and leave you in the lurch.

Failure to pay fees in accordance with the fee agreement is a typical reason for a lawyer's withdrawal. Moreover, if you don't pay your bills and your lawyer fires you as a client, he can keep your files and not give them to your new lawyer until you pay your bill.

Sample Retention Letter

Below is a form retention letter containing many variables that may apply:

Date

Name of Client
Address
Address

Dear Client:

This letter will confirm our fee arrangement for representing you in connection with the [DESCRIBE THE MATTER].

We will bill at our regular hourly rates in effect at the time the work is done. We revise our rates upward once a year. Attorneys' rates currently range from _____ to _____ per hour, depending on the experience of the attorney. _____ and I anticipate doing most of the work ourselves, but will use more junior lawyers and parale-gals to perform research, document review, and other tasks where appropriate. My current rate is _____ per hour; _____ current hourly rate is _____. Paralegals are charged at rates between _____ and _____, depending on experience.

We will bill you monthly for our time and disbursements. The bill will be itemized. It will show the date work is done, a short description of the work, the name of the person doing the work, the time spent, and the charge for the task. You agree to pay all bills within thirty days.

We have asked for an advance fee of $. We will charge our time and disbursements against the advance fee until it is exhausted. If it is exhausted we may request an additional advance fee in an amount which is appropriate in all the circumstances. **ALTERNATE:** We will retain this sum as security against payment of our final bill, or any bill which is unpaid after thirty days. **ALTERNATE:** You have agreed to pay us a minimum of $ per month, with adjustments made to reflect actual billings every six months.

We have not estimated the fees which may be charged in connection with this matter. **ALTERNATE:** You have asked us to estimate the fee which may be charged. We estimate the fee will be between $_____ and $_____. (Appropriate qualifying language should be added if an estimate has been made.)

VARIANT: The principals of a small business, an out of state business, or a new business may be asked to sign the fee agreement in addition to the nominal client. This may be appropriate where the client has no track record with us, or where there is no advance fee. In circumstances where the client cannot pay an advance fee, it may be appropriate to take a mortgage and note as security for our fee, and this should be described in the letter.

If our bills are not paid in accordance with this agreement, we reserve the right to withdraw from further representation, subject to the ethical rules governing attorneys. Our right to withdraw will depend upon the circumstances existing at the time we seek withdrawal, and we will not withdraw unless withdrawal can be accomplished in a manner consistent with the Rules of Professional Conduct. If an action is pending in court in which we are representing you, our ability to withdraw will be subject to the court granting us permission. The court has general supervisory authority over attorneys appearing before it. You will be given notice of the time and place where the court will hear any motion to withdraw that we may file.

ADD: [WAIVER OF AND CURRENT CONFLICT]

OPTIONAL - IF APPROPRIATE: As we have discussed, we represent many other companies and individuals. It is possible that some of our present or future clients will have disputes with [name of this client] during the time that we are representing [name of this client]. Therefore, as a condition to our undertaking this matter for you, you have agreed that this firm may continue to represent or may

continued

undertake in the future to represent existing or new clients in any matter that is not substantially related to our work for [name of this client], even if the interests of such clients in those other matters are directly adverse to [name of this client]. We agree, however, that your prospective consent to conflicting representation contained in the preceding sentence shall not apply in any instance where as the result of our representation of [name of this client] we have obtained sensitive, proprietary, or other confidential information of a non-public nature that, if known to any such other client of ours, could be used in any such other matter by such client to the material disadvantage of [name of this client].

ADD - IF APPROPRIATE [MULTIPLE CLIENT REPRESENTATION]

We have agreed to represent _____ in addition to your self/company. We have discussed this situation with you both, and based on what you have told us, we see no basis currently for any conflict of interest. It is on this basis that we have agreed to represent you both/all. However, it is conceivable that a situation will arise in the future where your interests will conflict. If that situation arises we have agreed that:

[1) deal with withdrawal vs. continuing to represent one of the group; 2) deal with the disclosure issue re confidences one to the other].

I trust this letter describes a satisfactory arrangement. Please sign and date below and return the original to me, [along with an advance fee of $_____.] A duplicate original is enclosed for your files.

We look forward to working with you on this matter.

Very truly yours,

Dewey, Cheatem & Howe
I agree to the arrangement described above.

Name_____

Date_____

Sample Billing Statement

Below is a sample billing statement containing information that law firm computers routinely generate for clients.

DEWEY, CHEATEM & HOWE

Pink, Panda & Co.February 26, 1995
801 Main Street
Jacksonville, CT 06987

STATEMENT D,C & H #123456

Our File #123.456   For Services Through February 26, 1995
General Representation

01/16/95 Review letter re trademark C. Benson .60 hrs. 145.00/hr	87.00
01/19/95 Office conference re trademark search. R. Fishman .20 hrs. 75.00/hr	15.00
01/19/95 Attention to trademark issue; office conference re same. C. Benson .30 hrs. 145.00/hr	43.50
01/20/95 Order trademark search; memo to file. R. Fishman .30 hrs. 75.00/hr	22.50
02/05/95 Attention to letter re trademark infringement; office conference re same. C. Benson .50 hrs. 145.00/hr	72.50

Fees for Legal Services $240.50

COSTS AND DISBURSEMENTS

02/08/95 Disclosure - Trademark Search	$127.15
Outside Delivery Services	13.36

Total Costs and Disbursements $140.51

TOTAL CURRENT BILLING FOR THIS FILE $381.01

An attorney's lien allows him to hold the files as collateral for your obligation to pay his fees.

This does not mean that you should simply pay every bill you get without question. You have the right to review in detail all of the bills you receive and inquire about inappropriate charges. In many cases, either the lawyer made a mistake on the bill or the client doesn't understand the work or how it relates to the case. These issues are usually resolved through reasonable discussion between lawyer and client. If you have a decent working relationship with your lawyer, you should be able to work out any fee dispute.

If you can't work out a fee dispute, you may need a new lawyer. If you do, talk with the new lawyer about resolving the dispute with your old one. If you don't need or want a new lawyer, you can also talk to your state bar association, which regulates lawyers. Many bar associations have procedures to assist clients in resolving fee disputes. Your local association should be able to provide information to you on this subject.

Firing Your Lawyer

You can fire your lawyer at any time for any reason. You need no justification. Simply advise her that she no longer represents you. So that everyone is clear on the termination, fire the lawyer in writing. However, if you haven't paid your bill, your ex-lawyer can sue you for unpaid fees. Just because you fire your lawyer doesn't mean that you don't have to pay a bill that you've already run up.

If you have a billing arrangement with a contingency-fee component, you may have to negotiate the amount of the fee for your prior lawyer. You should let your new lawyer work out how she will split the fee with the old lawyer. You should not have to pay more because you make a switch.

Though working with a lawyer may appear burdensome, it is usually a simple, relatively painless experience. Lawyers know that effective representation depends upon a solid partnership between lawyer and client. Consequently, most lawyers work to minimize tensions with their clients to ensure a smooth working relationship. If this relationship is established in your case, then both you and your lawyer are free to devote your attention to a united front against your adversary.

Getting Started: Filing a Lawsuit 6

A lawsuit begins when a plaintiff files a written complaint in court and "serves" it by delivering the document, along with a summons, to the defendant. The purpose of the complaint is to frame the dispute and notify the defendant of the precise claims against him. In starting a lawsuit, you should focus on the following issues:

1. Drafting a complaint that clearly articulates what you want and why you should get it

2. Including all related claims in the complaint

3. Including all plaintiffs and defendants who can and should be in the case

4. Picking the right court

5. Determining when to file the litigation

6. Serving the complaint on the defendant

Drafting the Complaint

The complaint is your first formal articulation of the claims against the defendant in the lawsuit. It should contain everything necessary to state a valid legal claim. If the jury believes everything in your complaint, you should win.

Though the plaintiff may on occasion prepare a "bare bones" complaint just to get the ball rolling, one usually prepares a complaint with the ultimate goal of persuading the defendant, the judge, and the jury that you will win. Though you probably discussed your claims with the defendant prior to filing the lawsuit in the hope of settling without litigation, filing a lawsuit raises the dispute to an entirely new level. The complaint should reflect your increased seriousness. A credible, persuasive complaint lets the defendant know that he has a fight on his hands.

A strong complaint is also important in communicating with the judge. The complaint will probably be one of the first documents the judge reads. Consequently, it may be your first chance to persuade the judge that you have good claims. Since persuasion and credibility are cumulative, and since a strong (or weak) beginning can influence the way the judge sees the rest of the case, you need to get off on the right foot. As in everything else, first impressions are lasting.

> "We shake papers at each other the way primitive tribes shake spears."
>
> —John Jay Osborn, Jr.

The complaint should set forth your claims in simple, concise, plain English. The necessary facts should be written in short, separate, numbered paragraphs, with each paragraph containing a single fact or set of circumstances. The complaint should also describe in detail the relief and remedies you seek. In sum, it should state precisely what you want and why you should get it.

Because of the importance of the complaint in developing credibility and persuading your audience, it should be long on facts and short on hyperbole. A complaint filled with claims of abhorrent and despicable conduct may be dismissed out of hand. Judges and lawyers have seen it all. For this reason, nouns and verbs are convincing, adjectives and adverbs are not. The complaint should read like Ernest Hemingway, not William Faulkner. As Joe Friday said on Dragnet, "Just the facts, ma'am." Since juries generally make decisions based on facts, not the rantings and ravings of lawyers, "just the facts" communicates that your case is strong.

Complaints generally follow a simple pattern. In the first paragraphs, they state the names of the parties, where they live, and other facts relating to the court's jurisdiction. The purpose of these paragraphs is to allege that the court has the power to decide the case. The complaint should next outline the key facts which, if true, are the basis of the claims. This portion of the complaint states who did what to whom. A complaint then generally sets forth each of the legal claims that arises out of the facts, such as breach of contract, negligence, or fraud. Complaints typically conclude with a request for relief, such as an award of monetary damages or an injunction. As discussed more fully in Chapter 8, you should also consider at this time whether you want a jury.

For example, in a suit on a debt, the complaint of the First National Bank of Boise first alleged that it and its borrower were from Boise. These paragraphs showed that the court in Boise should hear the case. The complaint then alleged that the defendant borrowed $100,000 from the bank but did not repay the loan. These paragraphs were the factual basis of the bank's claim. Next the complaint stated that the borrower's failure to repay was a breach of the loan contract, the legal claim in the case. Finally, the bank asked for relief, that it recover $100,000 in damages plus interest and attorneys' fees. These four sections made up the bank's simple complaint for breach of contract.

The Complaint Must Be Accurate

The allegations of the complaint must be true and accurate to the best of your belief. You can't make false claims against a defendant. Moreover, you can't negligently file unsubstantiated charges. Your facts must be based upon reasonable information and belief. Are there witnesses who will testify to the facts you allege? Do the documents say what you claim they do? You need to be able to prove that the facts in your complaint are true. If you haven't investigated the facts, or don't have a reasonable, informed, good-faith basis for your claims, don't file the litigation. In addition to subjecting yourself to a malicious prosecution claim, you can also be sanctioned by the court.

Joining Multiple Claims

You probably want to include all claims against the defendant in your complaint, provided that you outline each separately. In most jurisdictions, you should separate the claims from one another in separate counts. For example, Prentiss Porch Furniture manufactures patio furniture, which it sells through local retail stores, including Bill's Patio Supply. Prentiss sold a substantial volume of furniture to Bill's on credit in reliance upon Bill's financial statements. These statements represented that Bill's had enough money to pay its obligations. However, Bill's didn't and couldn't pay because it was broke. When Prentiss discovered that the financial statements falsely overstated Bill's assets and cash flow, it brought a lawsuit containing four separate counts, each arising out of the one sale.

In the first count, Prentiss sued for a breach of contract, claiming that Bill's didn't live up to its obligation to pay for the furniture. In the second and third counts, Prentiss sued for fraudulent and negligent misrepresentation, alleging that it sold the furniture to Bill's in reliance upon the false financial statements. Finally, Prentiss claimed that Bill's fraudulent acts were unfair and deceptive trade practices. Though factually similar to the fraud count, this claim was based on a specific statute regulating unfair trade practices.

Like Prentiss, you can join together in one lawsuit many different claims against the defendant. Indeed, you should join all claims based on the same set of facts. If you don't, you may be barred from bringing those claims later under principles of res judicata and collateral estoppel. *Res judicata* precludes a plaintiff from asserting claims that were decided in a prior lawsuit. *Collateral estoppel* blocks a plaintiff from relitigating facts or issues which were decided in a previous litigation. When these facts or issues are critical to claims made in a subsequent case, collateral estoppel can bar the suit in its entirety. Because of these principles, you make a mistake if you don't bring all claims arising out of the same events in one lawsuit.

Moreover, in order that all claims be resolved as efficiently as possible, you should probably join in one suit claims that arise out of different facts. The only reason not to join unrelated claims is concern that the case will become confusing. You can even join alternative and inconsistent claims, either of which, but not both, could be valid.

For example, in defense of Prentiss' lawsuit, Bill's could claim that there was no contract and, therefore, that Prentiss has no breach, of contract claim. In response, Prentiss could claim on the one hand that there was a contract and that Bill's is liable for its breach, or, in the alternative, that if there was no contract, then Bill's is liable for the value of the goods Prentiss shipped. In this type of "either/or" case, both claims cannot be valid at the same time, but either, if true, would allow Prentiss to recover damages from Bill's.

The bottom line is that you rarely go wrong in joining every claim you have in one lawsuit. If some claims need to be weeded out later, you can do so. If you leave out a claim, you can generally amend your complaint to add that claim later; however, you may not be able to add new claims late in the case when the defendant can argue that he is unable to prepare to defend the new claim. Therefore, it's safest to join all claims at the outset.

Who Can Sue and Be Sued

To be a party to a lawsuit, you must be the person who owns the claim or against whom the claim can be brought. Only the "real party in interest" can file litigation. If you are injured in an automobile accident, your spouse cannot file a lawsuit on your behalf because your spouse was not injured and does not own the claim. You must file the lawsuit in your own name. Similarly, the driver of the other car cannot sue your spouse. Rather, the driver must sue you.

There are certain exceptions to this rule. For example, children and incompetents are deemed unable to represent themselves because they lack sufficient capacity. Accordingly, they often have others represent them, such as parents, family members, guardians, or other fiduciaries.

Certain organizations also lack the capacity to sue or be sued. For example, a corporation typically has the right to be a plaintiff in a lawsuit only if it is qualified to do business, is properly licensed, has paid its taxes, and is otherwise in good standing. Corporations must meet these requirements in exchange for the privilege of using the courts to resolve their own disputes. Information on the status of corporations is maintained by the Secretary of State in most states and should be checked if you have questions.

Certain associations may not have the right to sue or be sued in their own names. For example, an unincorporated group of neighborhood homeowners may not be able to sue as an association because the association is not a separate legal entity. Since the association cannot act on behalf of the neighbors in court, the neighbors have to sue and be sued in their individual names. Partnerships are a hybrid in that you can probably sue both the partnership and the partners. Because the rules vary by state, you may need to research these capacity issues before filing suit.

Joining Multiple Parties

Before filing your lawsuit, consider whether you should join other plaintiffs or defendants in your case. When others have claims like yours, they may be able to be plaintiffs in your litigation. For example, in a bus accident case, many passengers, each of whom has separate claims, may be able to join together in one lawsuit against the bus company.

An advantage to plaintiffs joining together is that they can share lawyers, legal fees, and other litigation expenses. Depending on the number of plaintiffs, this can reduce significantly the cost of litigation per plaintiff. The downside, however, is that if all plaintiffs do not agree on strategies and tactics, conflicts can arise. If these conflicts become sufficiently severe, each plaintiff may need a separate lawyer, thereby eliminating most of the savings of being together in one case.

You may also join more than one defendant when the claims against each arise out of the same facts and there are common questions of law and fact. For example, in an automobile accident, if your car is hit by two other cars, you may be able to sue both drivers in one lawsuit.

Sometimes parties may be joined in a lawsuit who should not be part of the case. For example, if the claims against one defendant turn out to be so different from the claims against the others that the trial will be complicated or confusing, then that defendant should be dismissed from the case. If you want to pursue your claims against that defendant, you should do so in a separate lawsuit. However, you can still continue your lawsuit against the others. The typical remedy for misjoinder is to drop the party who does not belong, not to dismiss the case entirely.

Class Actions

In addition to filing a lawsuit, you can become a plaintiff by being a member of a class action. For example, David Johnson bought 100 shares of General Widget stock in 1989. In October, 1994, he received notice of a settlement of a class action which applied to all who bought General Widget stock in 1989. This notice explained that a lawsuit had been filed against the company by one plaintiff on behalf of all stock buyers, and that under the

Complaint Checklist

☐ Does it name the parties?

☐ Does it allege personal jurisdiction?

☐ Does it allege subject matter jurisdiction?

☐ Does it allege venue?

☐ Does it state the key facts?

☐ Is it specific enough?

☐ Does it allege an injury?

☐ Does it state all legal claims?

☐ Does it include all related claims?

☐ Does it include unrelated claims you want to assert?

☐ Does it include all potential defendants?

☐ Do you want a jury?

☐ Can you get a prejudgment remedy?

settlement, each purchaser would be paid $4.00 per share. In order to receive this money, David didn't have to file a lawsuit. He only had to send in his proof of purchase of the stock. Merely by electing not to exclude himself from the lawsuit, David became a member of a plaintiff's class action.

Class actions are filed by individual plaintiffs on behalf of large groups with similar claims. They are often filed in cases involving the sale of securities or large numbers of identical defective products. The "class representatives," the individuals who bring the cases, hire lawyers to represent them and the class as a whole. These lawyers are usually paid from any proceeds of a settlement or judgment. The rest of the money is then divided up among the class members. Through a class action, your claims may be asserted on your behalf without you knowing it. Only after you receive notice of the class action, often long after the case is filed, do you know that you can be part of the class.

Class members are not required to stay in the class; rather, when you receive a notice, you can join or opt out. If you join, then your claims are treated like those of everyone else in the class, and any judgment or release in the lawsuit binds you. Once you elect to stay in, you simply wait until the case is resolved and get what everyone else gets. If, on the other hand, you want to pursue your claims on your own, then you can opt out of the class. In this instance, you receive none of the benefits of the class action, and are not bound by any decision. Rather, you can pursue your own claims in your own lawsuit as if there was no class action.

For those with small claims, where the time and expense of litigation is often not worth the trouble, a class action may be the perfect vehicle for getting some compensation. Unless you have a significant individual case, it's usually a good idea to stay in the class.

Intervention

If you are not a plaintiff in a lawsuit but believe you should be, you can attempt to intervene. You can intervene as a matter of right if the litigation is over ownership of property in which you have an interest and the lawsuit may impair or impede your right to take possession of that property. For example, if two parties are litigating over ownership of land that you claim you own, you can intervene in their lawsuit to assert your right to the property.

Under the doctrine of permissive intervention, if you have claims arising out of the same facts as the existing lawsuit and the questions of law and fact relating to your claims are common to those in the main case, the court can allow you to join the case. This often happens in land-use disputes when a developer files a zoning application to construct a large project that affects many neighbors. If one neighbor challenges the application in court, other neighbors may be able to intervene to assert their rights in the one case.

Where to Sue

In addition to determining whom to sue and what to sue for, you must determine where to file the lawsuit. This question is largely governed by the legal concepts of jurisdiction and venue.

Subject Matter Jurisdiction

A court must have subject matter jurisdiction to decide your case. For example, federal district courts have the power to hear cases arising under federal law or between citizens of different states when the amount in dispute exceeds $50,000. Federal courts are not permitted to hear small, local cases, and this is the basis of the old adage that you shouldn't "make a federal case" out of a dispute. If you can't go to federal court, you have to go to state court.

If the federal court has jurisdiction, you can in most cases go to state court as well. In deciding where to go, you should compare the time it will take your case to get to trial, as well as differences in the pool of potential jurors, the likely judges, and the procedural rules and customs. Each court has strengths and weaknesses that can affect your decision to pick one or the other.

Many states have specialized courts to hear particular kinds of disputes. For example, probate courts resolve will contests, family courts hear child custody disputes, and traffic courts handle speeding tickets. Each specialized court has subject matter jurisdiction over a different category of cases. Since subject matter jurisdiction determines the fundamental power of a court to hear your claims, you must file your lawsuit in a court that has this jurisdiction over your type of dispute.

The rules on subject matter jurisdiction are specific by court and type of claim. Accordingly, check these rules before filing any lawsuit. If you file a case in a court that does not have subject matter jurisdiction over your claims, your case will be dismissed, and you will have wasted time and money.

Jurisdiction over the Defendant

In most cases, the court must also have jurisdiction over the defendant. Known as personal jurisdiction, this principle ensures that it is fair to force your opponent to defend the lawsuit in the state where you file. For example, a California businessman injured in a subway accident in New York City cannot sue the subway driver in California because California has no personal jurisdiction. This is because it would be unfair to require the driver, who does not live in and may never have been to California, to go there to defend himself in a lawsuit over an event that happened in New York.

The test for personal jurisdiction is whether the defendant has sufficient contacts with the state to make it fair to sue him there. Though personal jurisdiction is specific to each defendant, a plaintiff must establish that the defendant has "minimum contacts" with the state. The minimum contacts analysis involves a balancing of various factors, including where the defendant lives and where the events that give rise to the lawsuit occurred. In most cases, you sue the defendant where he lives and the "minimum contacts" are clear. It can get complicated, however.

For example, one summer in Yellowstone Park, a grizzly bear sprinted across the road. The Bickford family from Alabama jammed on the brakes of their car and came to a screeching halt. They were rear-ended by the Caldwell family from New Mexico, whose car was then hit by the Thompson family from Minnesota, which was then rammed by the Beckenstein family from Oregon. At least one passenger in each car was hurt, and each blamed the other drivers. Each plaintiff filed a lawsuit against the other drivers in their home states. All defendants asked the courts to dismiss the lawsuits because none of them lived or had ever even been in the states where the lawsuits were filed. In each case, the judge decided there was no personal jurisdiction and threw out the cases. Because the accident occurred in Yellowstone Park, Wyoming was the only state with a sufficient relationship to the accident and the defendants to be the proper place for the litigation. Accordingly, if any plaintiff wanted to sue all defendants in one case, he had to go to Wyoming. Because it wasn't worth the trouble to sue in Wyoming, none of the plaintiffs bothered to assert their claims. The inconvenience caused by personal jurisdiction rules caused the plaintiffs to give up their rights.

Jurisdiction over Property

When a dispute relates to a particular piece of property, the court may not need personal jurisdiction over the defendant. Rather, jurisdiction may exist where the property itself is located. For example, if many claim they own a piece of real estate, then regardless of where the individual claimants live, the court where the property is located would probably have jurisdiction to decide the case. Similarly, a suit to foreclose a mortgage should be filed in the jurisdiction where the property is located, regardless of where the plaintiff or defendant lives. This is because the suit relates to the property itself, not to claims the plaintiff and defendant have against each other personally.

Venue

Similar to personal jurisdiction is the concept of venue, which also concerns the location of the court where the plaintiff should file a lawsuit. However, unlike personal jurisdiction which mandates the state where litigation must be filed, venue rules dictate the proper county or geographical area within a state. For example, a New York City plaintiff should sue a Hartford, Connecticut defendant in Hartford, not Stamford, Connecticut. Even though personal jurisdiction would be proper in either city, venue rules require an out-of-state plaintiff to sue in the defendant's home county. Similarly, in a mortgage foreclosure, venue lies where the property is located, not where the plaintiff or defendant lives.

When to Sue

You may have to meet certain prerequisites before you can go to court. First, you must file your complaint before expiration of the applicable statute of limitations which precludes you from filing stale claims. Under the doctrine of exhaustion of remedies, you may also have to comply with administrative dispute resolution procedures before you can sue. For example, if you have a dispute with a failed bank that was taken over by the FDIC, you may have to file an administrative claim with the FDIC and wait 180 days before you can file litigation. The same is true with certain employment discrimination claims that you must file with federal or state administrative agencies before going to court. In a related vein, the parties can agree in a contract to pursue alternative dispute resolution procedures before instituting litigation. Some contracts, like customer agreements with stockbrokers and mutual funds or health insurance policies, require binding arbitration of disputes, which may preclude you from ever going to court. In order to avoid dismissal of your case, check to see whether the law or an agreement will delay or block your lawsuit.

Notifying the Defendant of the Lawsuit

When you file a lawsuit, the clerk of court issues a summons which you must give to the defendant. The summons advises the defendant of the time and place he must appear to defend himself. It, along with the complaint, must be served on the defendant to start the lawsuit.

"Service" is the term for delivering the summons and complaint to the defendant according to rules adopted to ensure that he knows that a lawsuit has been filed against him. Service is also the event that establishes jurisdiction over the defendant. The most traditional method of service is to have a sheriff hand the summons and complaint personally to the defendant. However, in most jurisdictions, "in-hand" service may be by any person over 18 years old. Additionally, some jurisdictions allow service by registered mail or by leaving the summons and complaint at the defendant's home with some other person who lives there.

When the defendant is an infant or incompetent person, each state has particular rules for service which you should review and follow.

When the defendant is a corporation, partnership, or other association, check the rules in each state for service of these entities. Corporations, for example, typically appoint an agent to accept service of a summons and complaint. Since agents should register with the Secretary of State where the corporation does business, the Secretary of State can usually identify the agent you should serve. Additionally, officers or other managing agents of a corporation are usually sufficient representatives to accept service.

Because some defendants attempt to avoid service or, at the very least, make it as difficult as possible, in many courts you can send written notice of the lawsuit to the defendant and request that he waive formal service. If the defendant refuses and makes you jump through hoops to serve him, then the court can charge him with your expenses. The purpose of this rule is to attempt to cut through some of the delay and expense of compliance with service rules.

Service is critical in that if you don't properly serve a defendant and the defendant does not voluntarily appear in court to defend

Service Checklist

Because a lawsuit does not begin unless properly served, you must comply with all service requirements. Consider the following:

- ☐ What documents must you serve?
- ☐ Do you have all necessary documents from the clerk?
- ☐ How must you serve them?
- ☐ Who must serve them?
- ☐ When must you serve them?
- ☐ Who must you serve?

himself, then any judgment you obtain is not enforceable. Consequently, the defendant will not have to pay you any money. It is as if you never filed the lawsuit.

When the defendant does not voluntarily waive service, you must prove to the court that you complied with all service rules. For example, you may be required to file a sworn affidavit signed by the sheriff or other person who served the defendant that would state, for example, "On March 18, I personally handed a copy of the summons and complaint to the defendant." This proof of service ensures that you can obtain a valid judgment and that the defendant will be liable to you.

Once you have filed and served the complaint and filed proof of service, you have done all you need to do to get the lawsuit rolling. The ball is now in the defendant's court.

FIRING BACK: RESPONDING TO THE SUIT

7

Alton Oil distributes home heating oil in the Northwest. It had a dispute over the price of oil with Gold Star, one of its suppliers. Alton believed that it was overbilled by $65,000 and refused to pay this additional charge. Alton called Gold Star a couple of times, assuming that they could work it out. Gold Star always said it would get back to Alton soon, but never called. Then, out of the blue, Gold Star sent a sheriff to Alton's door with a complaint that claimed not only that Alton owed $65,000, but also that it lied about its promise to pay for oil and committed unfair and deceptive trade practice. What for Alton had been a small misunderstanding over the price of oil became an assault on its character, integrity, and business practices. Alton was outraged at these false and scurrilous claims and was determined to fight.

Most who get sued feel Alton's outrage. Many defendants feel that a plaintiff's complaint is filled with lies or, at the very least, gross exaggerations. Two common but contrary reactions are to ignore the complaint as unworthy of response or to sue back for malicious prosecution. However, if you are properly served with a summons and complaint, you must defend yourself according to the rules of civil procedure.

The first step in any defense is to file an "appearance," ordinarily a single sheet of paper with the name, address, and phone number of your lawyer. By filing this document, the court knows that you have been served with a lawsuit, have received notice of the claims against you, and are ready to defend yourself. It also tells the court how to get ahold of you when necessary. Most important, it ensures that the court will not enter judgment against you without giving you advance warning.

You must also respond to the merits of plaintiff's claims. One option is to ask the judge to throw the case out of court for improper jurisdiction or venue, failure to serve you properly with the summons and complaint, or failure to state a valid claim against you. Another option is an answer, which is a written response in which you admit or deny the truth of the plaintiff's allegations, as appropriate. In addition, you may employ more offensive measures, such as filing your own claims against the plaintiff or others.

Regardless of the specific response you select, as with the plaintiff and his complaint, this is the first time you communicate officially with your opponent and the court in the context of the litigation. Consequently, your filing should send a message to your opponent and the court that you have a persuasive, credible defense and perhaps serious claims back against the plaintiff. Therefore, as with a complaint, be clear, factual and precise. Do not engage in hyperbole, which will be ignored by the judge and your opponent. In all of the following responses, you want to convey the impression that the plain, simple law and facts mandate a decision in your favor.

> "When you have no basis for an argument, abuse the plaintiff."
>
> —Cicero

Motions to Dismiss

If there are serious flaws in the plaintiff's complaint, you can file with the court a motion to dismiss—a request that the judge toss the plaintiff's case out of court. Traditional grounds for dismissal include lack of subject matter, personal or *in rem* jurisdiction, improper venue, failure to state a claim, or failure to issue or serve the summons and complaint properly. Since most judges believe that a plaintiff is entitled to his "day in court," you often file a motion to dismiss with two strikes against you. You may not want to file it unless your grounds are very strong.

Dismissal for Improper Service

Consider whether a motion to dismiss for improper service is simply wasting time and money by delaying the inevitable. If you win, the plaintiff can probably serve you again, unless he waits more than 120 days, and he will have to file a new lawsuit and get a new summons. Even this won't block the suit, unless the claim is barred by a statute of limitations because it is too old. In the last analysis, though a motion to dismiss may delay and irritate the plaintiff—which may give you some satisfaction—it may ultimately prove to be a waste of your time and money.

Dismissal for Lack of Jurisdiction

If you attempt to dismiss the case for lack of personal jurisdiction, be careful not to consent to jurisdiction by filing a general appearance. If you waive the personal jurisdiction defense, this court has the right to hear the entire case and render judgment for or against you. Therefore, if you want to assert this defense, make sure that your appearance states that it is for the limited purpose of contesting jurisdiction. This limited appearance avoids any argument.

Before you file a motion to dismiss for lack of personal or subject matter jurisdiction, consider alternative locations in which the plaintiff can refile the lawsuit. If you win, the plaintiff may file the case in another state or court that is worse than the first. Therefore, evaluate how litigation in those other courts effects the relative abilities of you and your opponent to pursue the litigation. You don't want to find yourself out of the frying pan and into the fire at the end of the day.

Dismissal for Failure to State a Claim

A complaint can be dismissed when the plaintiff fails to state a legal claim against you. In considering your argument, the judge will assume that everything the plaintiff says is true and then decide whether the plaintiff's best case scenario constitutes a valid claim. If the plaintiff can't plead a legitimate claim, then you should win.

You will probably think that the complaint doesn't state a claim and should be dismissed out of hand. More times than not, defendants think that a complaint is frivolous and that the judge should sanction the plaintiff. The judge, on the other hand, gives the plaintiff the benefit of every doubt, and the judge will be reluctant to grant your motion. Your motion could even backfire if the judge considers it a waste of time. This often happens because judges often assume that where there's smoke there's fire and that somewhere, somehow, a claim exists. For this reason, the judge may not devote as much attention to your motion as you think he should. Therefore, even if you think you're right, unless your argument is very simple and clear cut, a motion to dismiss may not be worth your while. The KISS—keep it simple, stupid—principle applies.

Response Checklist

- ☐ What is the response date?
- ☐ Was service proper?
- ☐ Were you served with all required documents?
- ☐ Is there personal jurisdiction?
- ☐ Is there subject matter jurisdiction?
- ☐ Is there venue?
- ☐ Do you understand the complaint?
- ☐ Does the complaint state a claim?
- ☐ Can you file a motion to dismiss?
- ☐ If the case is dismissed, what are the plaintiff's options?
- ☐ Are you better off with this lawsuit?
- ☐ Should you file an answer?
- ☐ Do you want a jury?

Motion for More Definite Statement

If you don't understand the plaintiff's complaint, you can move for a more definite statement of the claims. This request is proper when the complaint is so vague, ambiguous, or unclear that you can't respond. In making this request, outline for the judge why you don't understand the claims against you. Rather than dismiss the case, he can order the plaintiff to rewrite the complaint to clarify his allegations.

Answer

The most common response by a defendant is an answer. Similar to the complaint, the answer should state in simple, plain language whether you admit or deny each fact alleged in the complaint. It should respond paragraph by paragraph, fact by fact. If you believe that some facts in a paragraph are true, but others facts are not, then admit the portions that are true and deny the rest. If you do not know whether a fact is true, say you lack sufficient knowledge or information to admit or deny the fact, which is equivalent to a denial. Through the process, by the time the answer is filed, the parties should know the facts that are and are not contested.

Your answer is significant in that if you admit a fact, you are bound by that admission and can't later claim that the fact is not true, unless of course you amend your answer. Therefore, don't admit anything you're not sure about. You can't avoid admitting a known fact by claiming you don't know, however. Similarly, you can't duck admissions by refusing to investigate the facts or sticking your head in the sand. You have a duty to undertake a reasonable investigation of all the facts alleged in the complaint. For example, if the plaintiff alleges that you received a letter, you should review your files to see if you actually got it. You can't answer that you don't know without looking. Your duty to investigate is limited to facts within your control, however. You don't have to interview witnesses, collect documents from third parties, or otherwise research the plaintiff's case for him. Rather, you only have to search your own records and memory.

Finally, if the plaintiff didn't ask for a jury and you want one, request it with your answer. Review Chapter 8 as you consider whether you want a judge or jury to decide your case.

Affirmative Defenses

As part of your answer, you should state your affirmative defenses—those facts which enable you to win the case even if all of the plaintiff's allegations are true. For example, if the plaintiff waits too long to file his lawsuit, you should win under a statute of limitations, which precludes him from asserting old claims, even if the complaint otherwise states a valid claim. Similarly, a plaintiff cannot assert a claim that was discharged in the defendant's bankruptcy. Numerous other affirmative defenses are based on particular legal theories. Before filing an answer, determine whether any apply. Include them all in your answer. If you don't, you may be unable to rely upon them to defeat the plaintiff's claims.

Counterclaims

Since the best defense is often a good offense, in addition to filing an answer, you should file a counterclaim against the plaintiff if you have one. Though part of the plaintiff's case, a counterclaim is in effect a separate lawsuit filed by you. By filing a counterclaim, you wind up both a plaintiff and a defendant in the same case. Even if the plaintiff's complaint is dismissed, you can continue your counterclaim. A counterclaim is valuable in that it increases the risk of litigation for the plaintiff and may enhance your negotiating leverage in settlement discussions. If you plan to file one, you may want to review the preceding chapter on filing a lawsuit.

You can assert any claim as a counterclaim, regardless of its relationship to the plaintiff's claim against you. When your claim arises out of the same facts as the plaintiff's case, you have a compulsory counterclaim. If you don't assert it, then your claim may be barred in a separate, subsequent lawsuit because all related claims should be joined in the same case. Even if your counterclaim is not related enough to the plaintiff's claim that it is compulsory, you may want to include it anyway in order to resolve all disputes more efficiently in one case and to maximize your settlement position.

Cross-claims

In addition to a counterclaim against the plaintiff, you can file a cross-claim against any other defendant when that cross-claim arises out of the same transaction or occurrence as the plaintiff's suit against you. Similarly, these other defendants can file cross-claims against you. In multi-party accidents, for example, all of the defendants may sue one another through cross-claims. Similar to counterclaims, cross-claims are in effect separate lawsuits among the defendants which are merged with the main case.

Joining Other Parties

When you have claims against others that arise out of the same facts as the claims in the main case, you can join them in the

Answer Checklist

- ☐ Have you interviewed important witnesses?
- ☐ Have you reviewed important documents?
- ☐ Have you fully investigated the facts?
- ☐ Have you responded to each allegation?
- ☐ Have you denied every fact that is not true?
- ☐ Have you admitted any fact by mistake?
- ☐ Have you included all affirmative defenses?
- ☐ Do you have any counterclaims?
- ☐ Do you have any cross-claims?
- ☐ Do you want to join other parties?
- ☐ Have you included a jury demand?

lawsuit. For example, those who may be liable with the plaintiff on your counterclaim can become additional counterdefendants. Contributors, indemnitors, insurers, and others who may be liable to you for all or part of the amount you owe the plaintiff may also be joined as third-party defendants.

Joinder of other parties is limited by the same jurisdictional rules that apply to any lawsuit filed by a plaintiff in the first place in that a defendant cannot be forced to defend in a court that has no personal jurisdiction over him. If there is no personal jurisdiction over someone you want to join in a case, you may have to file a separate lawsuit in a court with proper jurisdiction.

Include Everything and Everybody

The principle underlying these rules is that all related claims and everyone who has responsibility for those claims should be brought into your lawsuit. This allows all disputes arising out of the same facts to be resolved in one place at one time, once and for all. This principle is perhaps best demonstrated by the multicar pileup.

For example, Frank Arnold was driving along I-95 in New York, which is three lanes across in either direction. Frank was in the passing lane. In the far right lane was a Baskin's Bread truck driven by Tom Elide. Without looking, Tom and Frank swerved into the center lane simultaneously and collided with each other. Frank bounced back into the left lane and jammed on his brakes. He was rear-ended by Clarence Chapman. Clarence's car bounced off of Frank's, helicoptered to the right and broadsided the Baskin's truck. All vehicles were damaged and all drivers were hurt.

The case began when Tom Elide sued Frank Arnold on the grounds that he was already in the middle lane when Frank negligently swerved into that lane without looking. Frank claimed that he was in the middle lane first and counterclaimed back against Tom. Moreover, since Frank wanted to make sure there was enough money to pay his damages, he joined Tom's employer, Baskin's Bread, as a counterdefendant on the theory that Baskin's was legally responsible for Tom's reckless driving. Since Clarence hit Frank in the same accident, Frank also brought in Clarence as an additional counterdefendant for negligently failing to stop in time to avoid the collision. Clarence responded by suing Frank on the grounds that nothing would have happened if it weren't for Frank's negligence. Clarence also sued Tom and Baskin's, claiming that they were also to blame for starting the whole chain of events. Tom then countersued Clarence because Clarence should have stopped. Since it owned the truck, Baskin's also sued Frank and Clarence for damage to the truck. In other words, everybody sued everybody else, and the jury was left to sort out who owed what to whom and why.

Though confusing, at least the whole mess was resolved in one case. The alternative—many separate lawsuits—would have been more time-consuming and expensive for the parties, and would have wasted much more court and jury time. For this reason, related claims should usually be resolved in one lawsuit.

PICKING YOUR AUDIENCE PART 1: JURY OR JUDGE

Amanda Peterson had four children, a substantial mortgage, car payments, and maxed-out credit cards. She was forced to work one and a half jobs in the local supermarket after her husband, Mark, was killed in a factory accident. She could barely keep her family or her nerves together.

Amanda sued Mark's employer, Sycamore Machine, for $15 million, claiming that Sycamore knowingly made Mark work on an unsafe assembly line. Amanda believes that if she wins, she will have a new life. If she loses, she will be miserable forever.

Amanda must pick either a judge or jury to decide her case. Amanda wants whomever she thinks will give her the most money. Her decision should be based on whom she thinks will best understand her problems and sympathize with her plight. She wants whomever will be caught up in the emotion of her story and want to make her life better. Making the right choice is critical to her success.

Can You Get a Jury?

You always have the right to trial by a judge. Jury trials are limited to lawsuits for money damages. Juries do not decide claims for injunctions or other types of non-monetary relief.

Juries may not decide certain categories of claims for money damages. For example, lawsuits brought under certain statutes or regulations adopted by a legislature or administrative agency must be presented to a judge. The laws themselves expressly preclude a jury trial.

You can also agree to waive your right to a jury trial in advance. Contracts often provide that all claims arising under them will be tried by a judge. For example, form loan documents and insurance policies often block you from submitting disputes to a jury. For these reasons, before you consider whether you want a judge or jury, determine whether you have a choice.

Sometimes a jury and a judge each rule on different parts of the same case. For example, in Margaret Dalton's case against Tom Dixon to stop the flow of the sewage into her yard, Margaret would ask the judge to force Tom to fix his septic system. She would submit her claim for damages to reimburse her expenses to the jury. At the end of the trial, the jury and judge would each decide their separate issues.

What Is a Jury?

A jury is a group of ordinary citizens from your community. This cross-section of society is theoretically able to hear and consider the evidence and render a just verdict. Because the jury is supposed to be a random sample selected from the local population, it is presumed to be fair and unbiased.

"It is the 'ordinariness' of the jury that finally emerges as its unique strength."

—Melvyn B. Zerman

How Does a Jury Decide a Case?

A jury sits patiently in the jury box throughout the trial, watching and listening to the two-act play performed by each side. Jurors cannot ask questions directly of the lawyers, witnesses, or the judge. They only perceive the evidence presented to them.

After hearing the evidence, the judge reads to the jury the applicable law in the form of jury instructions or jury charges. The jury is supposed to understand this law and then apply it to the evidence in the case.

After receiving its instructions, the jury retires to the jury room to deliberate in order to reach a verdict. In many states, the verdict must be unanimous. In civil cases in some states, a super majority of perhaps 75 percent must agree on a decision. If the jury can't agree, it is a "hung jury" and the case can be tried again to a new group of citizens. Because of the time and expense of a new trial, most judges make jurors deliberate long and hard before letting them leave without a verdict.

In deciding a case, theoretically the jury carefully reviews all of the evidence, considers the jury instructions, applies the law to the evidence and arrives at a reasoned decision. In practice, jurors can consider any legal, factual, ethical, or emotional factors they want. Notwithstanding this broad discretion, most experienced trial lawyers will tell you that juries are fair in most cases.

> "The average juror . . . wraps himself in civic virtue. He's a judge now. He tries to act the part and do the right thing."
>
> —Jacob D. Fuchsberg

Jury deliberations are secret. Neither the judge, the parties, nor anyone else is permitted to observe the jury's work. In order that the process be free of outside influence, jurors are not supposed to talk about the case to anyone during deliberations, including family and friends. They should not even speak to each other about the case unless they are in the jury room and in the presence of all jurors. Because of this secrecy, no one really knows what happens during the jury deliberations. Juries are free to do whatever they want, however they want. Litigants must rely on the good faith and civic responsibility of the jurors to render a just decision.

The Judge in a Jury Trial

The judge officiates a jury trial. Though he doesn't pick the winner and loser, he makes many decisions along the way. For example, he will exclude impermissible evidence or prohibit inappropriate arguments. Much like the referee in a football game, he makes sure that the litigants obey the rules and that the trial is fair to both sides.

Do You Want a Judge or Jury?

Many issues affect whether you want a judge or a jury. As you consider the following factors, keep in mind the principle that 6 or 12 heads are usually better than one. Even a judge cannot see and hear everything that happens in a trial. Too much goes on; attention spans are short. Every judge will miss something, and many will miss a lot. Because each juror may focus on something different, at least one of the people who decide your case will probably understand each point you make and communicate it to the others.

Moreover, though every judge is a lawyer, and many are wise and fair, judges have no monopoly on intelligence. Some are barely competent. Many are elected politicians. Others are selected by politicians based on their connections. Judges range from brilliant, experienced, former trial lawyers to those who rarely went to court before appointment to the bench. Disabuse yourself of the notion that donning a black robe invests an otherwise ordinary person with special wisdom. Juries often do a better job. With these principles in mind, consider the following issues in deciding whether you want a judge or jury.

> "I would rather have my fate in the hands of 23 representative citizens of the country than in the hands of a politically appointed judge."
>
> —Robert Morgenthau

Complexity of the Legal Issues

Are the legal claims and defenses in the case black and white or shades of gray? Are they simple or complex? Will the jury understand the law it is supposed to apply? Does a strict application of the law lead to a fair and just result?

The conventional wisdom is that juries are better with simple legal issues and judges are better as the facts become more complex. In reality, most legal issues can be reduced to simple, basic principles that any jury can understand.

> "It has been said that a judge is a member of the Bar who once knew a governor."
>
> —Curtis Bok

A jury may be more unpredictable when a strict application of the law might lead to an unjust result. A judge, who is a trained lawyer with an appellate court looking over his shoulder, is more likely to decide a case based on legal principles, regardless of intrinsic fairness. For example, Sycamore Machine might believe that even if it did nothing wrong, a jury would give Amanda Peterson some money in sympathy, and a judge would more likely rule in its favor.

If your facts are bad, but you have good legal defenses, go for the judge. If the reverse is true, pick a jury.

How Complex Are the Facts?

Is your case a simple fender bender or a complex antitrust case? Do you have an easy explanation for why your financial statements appear misleading? Is your case outside of the jury's ordinary experience, or will they grasp it easily? The conventional wisdom is that if you have the simple side of the case, you want a jury. If your arguments cannot be presented clearly and concisely, or if you have too much to explain away, you want a judge. As with legal issues, the ability of a jury to analyze and understand complex facts is often underestimated. If your act in the play is properly produced and directed, the average jury should understand you as well as the average judge.

> "I never saw twelve men in my life, that, if you could get them to understand a human case, were not true and right."
>
> —Clarence Darrow

Who Is the Judge?

In many states and most federal courts, one judge handles your case from beginning to end. Investigate the strengths, weaknesses, experiences, and biases of the judge. Some judges trained as insurance defense lawyers, and they've seen every plaintiff's excuse in the world. Others were plaintiff's employment lawyers who believe the big company is usually wrong. Some have bleeding hearts; others are cold as ice. Some listen attentively; others sleep through a trial. Some know the rules of evidence; others don't have a clue. Before you pick a judge to decide your case, know where he's coming from. Consider carefully whether the themes of your case will resonate with him.

> "I don't want to know what the law is; I want to know who the judge is."
>
> —Roy M. Cohn

When a judge is not assigned to the case until just before trial, evaluate the pool of likely judges. Though you don't know exactly who he will be, there may be a small universe of potential judges. Evaluate the strengths and weaknesses of each and the odds of getting a good or bad one. Balance these probabilities with the jury you are likely to get.

Who Will Be on the Jury?

The jurors who will decide your case all live in the same city, county, or other geographic area. In predicting the composition of the jury, assume a cross-section of the community. Evaluate the experiences and biases of the likely jury pool. For example, a jury in Russell, Kansas should have a higher percentage of conservative, white farmers than a jury from the South Bronx. A jury in Palm Springs may be older than a jury in Venice Beach. O. J. Simpson's Los Angeles criminal trial jury was predominantly black; his Santa Monica civil trial jury was predominantly white. Juries in some jurisdictions are known for big verdicts. Others are renowned for tightfistedness. Evaluate the extent to which your theme will ring true with the likely jury.

Though the jury pool may be a representative sample, you should assume that the jury will be older than a cross-section of adults—principally because many younger citizens are excused for work, child care, or other reasons. Of course, if age is an issue in the case, remember that judges usually have a fair amount of gray hair as well.

How Emotional Is the Case?

Civil litigation ranges from the dry, boring, breach-of-contract case between two substantial businesses to gut-wrenching claims like Amanda Peterson's. Consider whether the jury will feel compassion, sympathy, or sorrow for one side or the other, or if it will not care. As a general rule, most plaintiffs with highly charged claims want a jury in the hope that the jury will be swept away in a tide of emotion and award huge damages. However, a judge may also have a soft spot for one kind of plaintiff and render a substantial verdict. You should attempt to predict how the emotions in the case will affect the likely judge or jury making your decision.

Who Are the Parties?

Are you more or less sympathetic than your opponent? Is the dispute between two large corporations, or is it David versus Goliath? Are you a wealthy businessman or just trying to make

Judge or Jury Checklist

- ☐ Who will be your judge?
- ☐ Who will be on your jury?
- ☐ How good are the facts?
- ☐ How complex are the facts?
- ☐ Do you have a simple factual argument?
- ☐ How good is the law?
- ☐ How complex is the law?
- ☐ Do you have a simple legal argument?
- ☐ How emotional is the case?
- ☐ Who do the emotions favor?
- ☐ Who is more sympathetic?
- ☐ Who will the judge or jury best identify with?

ends meet? Evaluate the relative sympathies that you and your opponent will engender and whether they play better in front of a judge or jury.

How Do You Request a Jury?

In most jurisdictions, you don't get a jury trial unless you ask for one. The written demand for a jury trial should be filed with the court. Though procedures vary, you generally must ask for a jury trial early in the case. Most lawyers request a jury when they file their complaint or answer.

If you select a jury and then change your mind, you can usually request a trial by judge. However, if you want to switch, you may have to get your opponent's consent. If one of you has a right to a jury trial, then both of you usually do. Once one side requests a jury, then all must consent to a change.

CIVIL LITIGATION: 9
THE BASICS

The court system has its share of rules and customs that dictate what happens in a lawsuit. To understand litigation fully, you need to know some of the basics of judicial procedure and bureaucracy. These basics include how to know when to do what and how to deal with the court.

Managing the Flow

Although litigation may at times appear a state of anarchy, the process flows in a fairly predictable pattern, from filing a lawsuit through discovery and eventually trial. Though something unusual always happens, the overall structure of each case is consistent. This pattern is based on the rules, orders, and procedures that regulate the steps necessary to move a case through trial.

Rules of Civil Procedure

Federal and state courts have rules of civil procedure which govern virtually every aspect of a case from beginning to end. These rules cover requests to the judge, filing and serving documents, discovery, trials, and judgments. Almost everything you do in a case is affected by a rule. Though lawyers miss or ignore these rules on a regular basis, check them before you do anything to make sure that you comply. If you breach the procedures, at the very least you look sloppy or unprofessional, which reduces your credibility and ability to persuade. If your breach is significant, the judge can sanction you.

Local Rules

In addition to federal and state rules, individual judicial districts and even courts have their own local rules that amplify or modify the broader regulations. Local rules reflect the needs and desires of the local judges and lawyers. Some local rules, and particularly those in federal district courts, are quite broad and apply to many aspects of civil litigation. For example, they contain time requirements and deadlines, rules for filing documents, provisions for conferences with the judge, and regulations on lawyer conduct.

Court Orders

In addition to rules of civil procedure, judges often enter orders in cases which dictate the course of a lawsuit. They contain deadlines for amending complaints and answers, joining new parties, joining new claims, and conducting discovery. These orders, like the rules themselves, can be amended by a request to the judge but should not be ignored.

Planning Conferences

Many judges hold at various times during the case planning or status conferences to help the parties work through the dispute as efficiently as possible. At the initial conference, you will probably discuss with the judge the facts of the case and the issues in dispute. The judge may help you try to resolve extraneous issues to reduce the scope of the dispute. You will also probably discuss the amount of discovery each side needs, including the number of depositions. Deadlines may be set for discovery, amending pleadings, and for other steps in the process. You may even pick a date for trial. Invariably, the judge will also encourage you not to waste time and money on litigation but instead to settle the case. The judge may even refer you to another judge for a settlement conference.

The status conference may be the first and one of the few times you can talk openly with the judge about the case. These conferences usually take place around a table in the judge's office, known as his "chambers." The judge will often tell jokes and war stories. He and the lawyers may discuss other cases or simply chew the fat for a while. Thereafter, everyone may have an informal dialogue about your case. Take advantage of this process. Particularly in jurisdictions which assign one judge to a case for its entirety, use the status conference not only to discuss dates and procedures but to argue your case. This conference can be an excellent opportunity to continue the process of persuading the judge that you are right and your opponent is wrong.

Motion Practice

A motion is a request that the court do something. You "move" the court to make your opponent give you documents in discovery or allow you an extra 30 days to file your answer to the complaint, for example. Although not always, motions are usually in writing. Motions must be filed for virtually anything you want the judge to do in your case.

Evidentiary Support for Motions

Motions that do not relate to purely legal or procedural issues must be supported by evidence—facts that can be considered by the court in deciding the motion. Rather than hold an evidentiary hearing with witnesses and exhibits, written evidence is often submitted. For example, copies of transcripts of depositions, answers to interrogatories, and documents produced by your opponent in discovery are often used (see Chapter 10 for more on these documents). You can also file affidavits.

An affidavit sets out in numbered paragraphs the facts you believe the court needs to consider in deciding a motion. For example, if you can't attend a deposition because you will be recovering from back surgery, you can file an affidavit explaining your health problems and perhaps attach to it your medical records or a note from your doctor. Because you sign the affidavit under oath and penalty of perjury, the court is able to rely on the facts in the affidavit in deciding the motion.

Arguing Motions

Unless your opponent consents to the motion, you will probably need to argue to the judge. Accordingly, a contested motion is usually supported by memorandum, often known as a brief, in which you argue in writing why you should win. Your opponent then files a reply brief arguing his side of the case.

Depending on the court and the significance of the motion, the judge may want to hear the lawyers argue in person. As with everything else in litigation, the key to oral argument is

"When you have the facts on your side, argue the facts. When you have the law on your side, argue the law. When you have neither, holler."

—Albert Gore, Jr.

credibility with the judge. Accordingly, arguments should be direct and to the point. Again, the KISS—keep it simple, stupid—principle applies. If the judge doesn't understand what you're talking about each step of the way, he will lose confidence in your position and you will not persuade him.

More important, if the judge asks you a question, be direct and to the point in your answer. Many lawyers beat around the bush rather than admit weaknesses in their positions. By and large, evasive answers are damaging. Most judges can see through them in a second. You are much better off admitting the negative, thereby enhancing your credibility, and moving on to highlight the strengths of your position.

You also want to be succinct in your argument. Some lawyers repeat the same argument time and again, which does little more than blunt its effectiveness. It may also cause the judge to wonder whether you think he's stupid. Also resist the impulse to respond to every argument of your opponent, particularly if you've covered it earlier. Two lawyers going back and forth in an attempt to have the last word looks ridiculous. If your argument is clear, the judge will remember it.

Judge: "Are you trying to show contempt for the court?"

Flower Belle Lee: "No, I'm doing my best to hide it."

—W. C. Fields and Mae West in *My Little Chickadee*

Briefs

Briefs outline the factual and legal arguments which support your position. Like complaints, answers, and other written documents filed with the court, briefs should be direct, concise, and in plain English. Though you need to be clear, you do not need to be repetitious. Overreaching arguments generally do not win the day. To the contrary, they can diminish your credibility. Be professional and precise at all times.

A defense attorney imprecisely used the word "dreck" to describe his opponent's brief. Though he thought it was a generic derogatory term for rubbish, he failed to appreciate that it is also in Yiddish an expletive meaning excrement. This misuse set off a firestorm of legal paper which resulted in a court order threatening sanctions for inappropriate language. The moral of this story is don't be cute and refrain from using words you don't know.

The judge is not the only audience for your brief. In addition to your opponent, the law clerks who work for many judges are critical members of your audience. They are usually recent law school graduates with little or no practical litigation experience, and as such they probably have minimal knowledge of the legal and factual issues in your case. Since judges rely on their clerks in varying degrees to review and analyze the law and the facts and draft decisions, briefs should be written with the assumption that the audience is starting from ground zero. Even if the judge has no clerk or takes the laboring oar himself, he considers many different kinds of cases and may not retain a working knowledge of the relevant law. Consequently, don't assume much prior knowledge in writing your brief.

> "Whether we are trying a case, writing a brief, drafting a contract, or negotiating with an adversary, words are the only things we have to work with."
>
> —Charles Allen Wright

You can usually reply to your opponent's brief. If you've already filed your own, do not reargue your position. You may only irritate the judge by repeating yourself. You may also want to resist the urge to respond to every insignificant point your adversary makes. Since you want to be direct, simple, and to the point, respond only to those arguments likely to affect the judge's decision.

Applying the Law

Briefs are the principal means of communicating the law to the court. Under our system, the law is comprised primarily of statutes and decisions from prior cases. Statutes are specific rules of law adopted by legislatures. These laws provide, for example, that you shall not drive over 55 miles per hour on state highways.

Of perhaps greater importance in civil litigation are decisions of judges in earlier cases. Our law is based on the legal principles of English common law that have evolved over the centuries. These laws are found in published opinions from prior cases. Judges rely on these opinions as precedent in interpreting legal issues in your case. A key to successful argument is to find other cases that are similar to yours and argue to the judge that she should do the same thing in your case. Since every case is different, a goal in writing the brief is to convince the judge that the decisions you cite are better precedent than your opponent's.

It's also important to cite persuasive cases. Some cases are much better reasoned than others. Indeed, you can find an opinion to support almost any legal proposition. For this reason, a well-analyzed case is more persuasive than a flawed one. The court issuing the decision also makes a difference. For example, a federal appellate court opinion will influence a federal trial judge in New York far more than a Nevada trial court decision.

Motions for Extensions of Time

The most common motion in the American judicial system is for extension of time. As you go through your lawsuit, very few things will happen on schedule. This will be a source of great frustration for you; however, it is a fact of life that you cannot avoid.

> "An incompetent attorney can delay a trial for years or months. A competent attorney can delay one even longer."
>
> —Evelle J. Younger

Many clients ask their lawyers to file objections to motions for extension of time, even if it's the first request. This tactic is generally not worth your trouble because the judge will probably grant the extension and may think that you are uncooperative. Moreover, the law of the jungle in litigation means that the "eye for an eye, tooth for a tooth" rule applies. If you are unreasonable in opposing a motion for extensions of time, your adversary will be equally unreasonable when you need more time. Therefore, in order for the litigation process to work as smoothly as possible, you should probably consent to reasonable requests for extensions of time.

Motions to Amend

Another common motion is to amend. If you discover new facts or identify new claims, you can ask the court to allow you to modify your filings to reflect these changed circumstances. Unless amendment will unfairly burden your opponent's preparation of the case or is filed just before trial, it should be allowed.

Dispositive Motions

A dispositive motion is a request that the judge decide the case before trial. The most common is the motion for summary judgment. Since summary judgment allows you to avoid the time and expense of trial, you should consider filing this kind of motion in every case.

A motion for summary judgment is appropriate when no factual issues exist in the case. The job of the jury is to resolve the disputed facts to find the "truth." Absent a "genuine issue of material fact" and a dispute as to the "truth," the only issue in the case is application of the law to the undisputed facts, which is always an issue for the judge. In these cases, the jury has nothing to decide. The judge should grant summary judgment.

Summary judgment is often granted in loan collection actions. When a borrower doesn't pay, the bank typically sues to recover the debt. Everyone knows that the borrower didn't pay and is simply stalling. Since nonpayment is an undisputed fact, the jury is not asked to decide that issue at a trial. Rather, the judge issues summary judgment for the bank and the case ends.

As with motions to dismiss, many judges are reluctant to grant summary judgment even when they should. Unless you have a clear, simple argument, summary judgment may not be worth the cost of preparing the motion. Even if you can't get summary judgment on all claims, partial summary judgment on some of the counts can shorten the trial. By weeding out some of the claims, you are able to focus more directly on the key claims in the case.

Stipulations

Another way to limit the factual issues decided at trial is through a stipulation or an agreement between the plaintiff and defendant that certain facts are true for purposes of the trial. The jury must accept these facts and cannot decide the case contrary to them. By reducing the facts in dispute, a stipulation can potentially shorten the trial.

DISCOVERY: LEARNING YOUR OPPONENT'S CASE

10

John Thompson sued Midnight Investments because a penny stock he bought over the phone dropped from $55 to $3.25 two weeks later. John claimed that Midnight manipulated the stock price up and then unloaded its shares at a huge profit, leaving John holding the bag. John requested all of Midnight's documents relating to nine-penny stocks it was manipulating. He also asked for records concerning other investors who shared his fate. Midnight had no objection and told John he could look at the records at any time. They were among 3.5 million pieces of paper stored in an old, unheated warehouse that reeked with the smell of tobacco formerly stored there. John spent many miserable days sorting through documents in the process known as discovery.

In discovery, the parties exchange the facts that relate to their cases. You may be forced to respond to written questions, hand over all of your documents, surrender data stored on your computer and answer deposition questions for hours and perhaps days. You should also learn all of the facts that relate to your opponent's position and perhaps much more. Finally, you can use discovery to define and limit the legal and factual issues for trial.

The underlying purpose of discovery is to allow each side to learn everything necessary to make its best case. Discovery is largely a preview of your opponent's act in the trial play. This preview enables you to undermine your adversary's production. By narrowing the issues, discovery also lets you pare down your presentation. Moreover, it educates both parties enough about the other's strengths and weaknesses so that there's a better chance to settle the case before trial. However, because discovery is so broad and can be so time-consuming and expensive, its burdens often exceed its benefits.

Discovery Procedures

There are four key discovery procedures—interrogatories, requests for production of documents, requests for admissions, and depositions.

Interrogatories

Interrogatories are written questions to your opponent that solicit information on any subject that relates to the case. They must be answered under oath—a promise to tell the truth—and penalty of perjury. For example, you can ask your adversary to identify all people who know anything about the case, state all facts that relate to his claims, or explain how he calculates his damages. Interrogatories force your opponent to describe in general terms his view of the world and identify the people who know the facts that support that view. You can also ask your opponent questions, which require him to review and analyze his information, that may help prove your case. For example, you can ask him to list his sales by month, product, and customer. While this strategy can shift much of the work to your adversary, he can and should respond simply by producing the documents that contain the information to force you to do all of the analysis yourself.

Requests for Production of Documents

You should submit with your interrogatories a request that your opponent produce for your review all documents that relate to the case, including writings, photographs, computer records, and any other information stored in electronic devices. To review these documents, send a list of the specific documents or categories of documents that you want to look at. Make sure that your request is thorough. You don't want to be surprised at trial by a key document that you didn't ask for. But, be as narrow and specific as possible. Don't be like John Thompson and ask for everything or you may get it. Very broad document requests often feed into the tactic of producing mountains of material in the hope that you will miss the few key items buried in the mass.

Such requests are critical in that documents describe what happened while it was occurring. Unlike witness memories, the story told by documents doesn't change over time. For example, notes of conversations and meetings are often the best proof of who said what to whom. Because of their reliability, the side with the best documents often wins.

When you produce documents, you are required to identify them as responsive to a particular request or produce them as they are ordinarily kept in your files so that your opponent can figure out what they are. Though a favorite trick of some lawyers, you are not allowed to shuffle them like a deck of cards to make them hard to understand or to hide a "smoking gun" in boxes of irrelevant paper.

Requests for Admissions

These are written requests that your opponent admit the truth of certain facts or the application of law to facts. Though underutilized, these requests effectively streamline a case.

For example, if a bank sues a borrower who doesn't pay back his loan, the bank can ask the borrower to admit that he signed a promissory note, that the copy of the note attached to the request is genuine, and that he owes $100,000 to the bank. If the defendant admits these facts, then the bank does not have to present witnesses at trial to prove that the defendant executed the note and owes $100,000. The bank proves its case through responses to the requests. You should use these requests to get your adversary to admit as much as possible in order to reduce your work at trial.

The natural reaction of any person served with requests for admissions is to deny all bad facts. Certainly the defaulting borrower would want to deny that he owes $100,000 because he would lose all negotiating leverage. However, if you don't admit a fact that you should, as a penalty you may have to pay your opponent's legal fees and expenses in proving that fact at trial. Though in the bank's case the penalty might not be much, if your opponent has to fly in an expert witness from out of town for two days of testimony, the costs could be significant.

Depositions

A deposition is an opportunity to take testimony before trial of your opponent or any one else. In a deposition, a lawyer asks questions and a witness answers. The witness testifies under oath and the penalty of perjury. A court reporter takes down the questions and answers and prepares a transcript. A deposition is like court testimony except that it ordinarily takes place in a lawyer's conference room.

To take a deposition, you simply send to all parties a written notice of the time and place and the identity of the person you plan to depose. If the deponent is a party in the case, the notice is sufficient to compel the person to appear. If he is not a party, then you should also serve a subpoena. A subpoena is a form issued by an attorney and served by a sheriff, or in some jurisdictions, anyone over 18 years old. You must include a witness fee and mileage money with the subpoena. If you don't subpoena a witness and he doesn't show up, you may be required to pay your adversary's costs in preparing for and attending the deposition. Therefore, be cautious about a nonparty's promise to appear without a subpoena.

In many jurisdictions, you cannot compel a non-party witness to go to a deposition more than 100 miles away, as the crow flies. In other jurisdictions, you cannot force a deponent to leave his home county. If the witness is too far away, you have to go to him.

You can also request that a deponent bring documents to the deposition. If he is not a party, use a subpoena *duces tecum* to compel production. It is just like a request for production of documents which is served on a party.

Depositions are typically taken for two purposes. In most cases, they are part of the discovery process. You take your opponent's deposition to find out the facts he knows which have bearing on the case—good or bad, to see how effective a witness he will be at trial and to pin him down on key facts so he can't change his story. If your opponent changes his story at trial, then you can use the deposition for cross-examination.

Deposition testimony can also be used as a substitute for trial testimony. Particularly when a witness lives too far away from the court or may not be alive when the trial occurs, a deposition can be used instead of live testimony. Someone else reads the transcript at trial as if he were the witness. You can also videotape the deposition so that the testimony appears more like the real thing. Moreover, if you are a party to a case, or a senior employee of a corporate party, even if you are present in court, your deposition testimony can be read to the jury. For this reason, if you are a party, you should assume that your entire deposition testimony may be used against you at trial. Because of their importance, deposition strategies are discussed in the next chapter.

Investigation

Nothing prevents you from interviewing a nonparty witness at any time or from looking at his documents. You don't even need to tell your adversary that you are doing this investigation. Learning information that you don't have to share with your opponent can give you an advantage at trial. Before you depose a nonparty witness, give him a call to see what information you can get informally.

Mandatory Discovery

In some jurisdictions, and particularly in some federal courts, discovery is mandatory. For example, you may be required to disclose early in the case the identity of all people who have relevant evidence and your damages calculations. You may also need to produce all relevant documents.

In addition, many courts have rules requiring disclosure of expert witnesses in advance of trial. For example, you may have to name your expert, describe the substance of his opinion and the facts on which that opinion is based, and produce his expert report. If you fail to comply with these expert disclosure rules, the judge may not allow your expert to testify.

Time for Discovery

Discovery generally commences shortly after the defendant files his answer to the complaint. Because answers to interrogatories and produced documents are often used to prepare for depositions, the parties typically pursue these discovery procedures first. Moreover, since you usually want to ask a witness about her documents, you rarely want to take depositions before you get them.

In many courts, timing is dictated by the parties. Forty-five days after service of the complaint, you can take whatever discovery you want whenever you want. If you seek a preliminary injunction or have some other need for expedited discovery, you can ask the court to begin immediately. Some courts require the parties to meet shortly after a lawsuit is filed to discuss the timing of discovery. They then submit a discovery plan which is often approved by the judge. Sometimes the judge issues an order on

Discovery Checklist

You should prepare a comprehensive and efficient discovery plan. There are many discovery procedures that can be used for different purposes. All of them cost money; depositions cost the most. As you create a discovery plan, evaluate the information you hope to get, how much you need it, how much it will cost to get it, and whether it's worth the time and effort. In developing the plan, consider the following:

- ☐ Your opponent's documents
- ☐ Your documents
- ☐ Documents from third parties
- ☐ All people with knowledge of the facts
- ☐ What each of them may know
- ☐ Expert witnesses
- ☐ The discovery procedures you can use to get the information
- ☐ Whether you can find out the information informally on your own
- ☐ Who you need to depose
- ☐ Whether your opponent will take the deposition if you don't
- ☐ The relative benefits of the deposition
- ☐ How much the deposition will cost
- ☐ Whether there are reasonable alternatives to the deposition
- ☐ Whether requests for admission can narrow the case

his own that dictates the time for discovery. Pay attention to discovery deadlines. Though you can often get extensions, if you let the deadlines slip, you may not be able to take important discovery you need.

Scope of Discovery

Discovery is very, very broad. Not only are you required to disclose information which is relevant to the claims in the case; you must also disclose information that is reasonably calculated to lead to the discovery of admissible evidence. As a practical matter, almost anything goes. For this reason, the parties are permitted to go on fishing expeditions to discover virtually anything they want.

You are only required to produce information in your custody or control. If you are an individual, you should provide data that you or your agent have. A corporation must produce information retained by its employees or others acting at its direction and control. However, you don't have to do your opponent's investigation for him by searching out information from others. For example, if your opponent asks for your bank records and you don't keep them, you don't have to get them from your bank. Your opponent can go to the bank as easily as you can, and, under the rules of discovery, is required to do so.

Objections to Discovery

You will probably think that many of your opponent's discovery requests are way out of line. You may assume that they are for the sole purpose of making you spend lots of time and money assembling irrelevant information. Because of the broad scope of discovery, your relevance objection will probably not prevail. There are certain objections which may work, however. The most common are as follows:

Privileged Information

You are not required to disclose information that is privileged under the rules of evidence. For example, you should not disclose conversations, letters, memoranda, and other communications between you and your lawyer.

You should also withhold information prepared in anticipation of litigation. For example, your opponent can't discover your notes of witness interviews or your analysis of the claims and defenses in the case. The purpose of this work-product privilege is to prevent your opponent from using your investigation and analysis against you and to allow you to prepare your act in the play the way you want to.

If documents are privileged, you will probably have to prepare a privilege log which describes in general terms the documents you withhold. The purpose of this log is to allow your opponent to evaluate the validity of the privilege and, if necessary, ask the court to order you to produce the documents. If a dispute over privilege arises, the judge will decide whether it's valid.

If you disclose privileged documents in error and catch your mistake, an ethical opponent should give them back without reading or copying them. Since every lawyer knows of situations where the adverse lawyer wrongfully copied and kept a privileged document mistakenly produced, be careful that you segregate all privileged materials from your document production.

Undue Burden

An underlying theme of discovery is cost. Legal fees mount quickly as lawyers and paralegals review boxes of documents and attend depositions. Though rarely admitted, part of the discovery game is to make life unpleasant for the adversary. Your opponent may request volumes of documents that are difficult to assemble just to make you work hard. If this happens, ask him to do the hard work. For example, if you contend that an insurance company failed to pay your claim, and you ask to review the company's tens of thousands of other claim files, the company can object to delivering the documents to you but invite you to travel to its document warehouses around the country to look at the files yourself. Similarly, a California defendant in a New York lawsuit can object to his deposition in Manhattan because it is unfair to make the defendant, who did not pick the court, travel for his deposition.

Vagueness

If you don't understand a discovery request, object on the grounds of vagueness. Make your adversary reframe the question. A better response is to reframe the question yourself. By asking and answering your own question, you give your opponent the information you want, not what he wants.

Confidential Information

Particularly in business cases, one side may seek confidential business information of the other. In other cases, parties seek employment files of key witnesses that may be confidential by statute. These requests invariably draw an objection. However, confidentiality in and of itself is not a basis for withholding information. Rather, this information is usually disclosed pursuant to a protective order which specifically restricts the people who can see the information and the ways they can use it.

Discovery Disputes

Discovery is in part a negotiation. Many lawyers make aggressive objections with the expectation that they will serve as bargaining chips when the parties negotiate who will produce what for whom. Other times objections are made simply to obstruct or delay. Whatever the reason, you and your opponent will inevitably become embroiled in a discovery dispute. Since in most jurisdictions the lawyers are required to negotiate these disputes in good faith before going to court, this negotiation becomes part of the discovery ritual. Through it, you can test your opponent's resolve and negotiating skills. You can also probe the theories your adversary will rely on to make his case.

If the lawyers can't work out a dispute, then the party seeking discovery can file a motion to compel production of the information. The party attempting to block the discovery can file a motion for a protective order. Either or both of these motions gets the dispute before the court. The judge then decides whether and to what extent discovery is appropriate. For example, he can order that you receive some but not all of the documents you request. Or, he can order that you pay your adversary's costs in traveling to your hometown for a deposition.

Failure to Comply with Discovery

If you fail to comply with a court order compelling discovery, you can be sanctioned. You may suffer the same fate if you fail to show up at a deposition or do not respond to discovery requests. Sanctions range from an order that you pay your opponent's attorney's fees to dismissal of your case. Moreover, regardless of the magnitude of the sanctions, you will look bad in front of the judge and diminish your credibility. You should comply with all discovery orders to make sure that you don't get on the judge's wrong side.

Why Does Discovery Take So Long and Cost So much?

Because discovery is so broad and open-ended, it can take on a life of its own. In a business case, the parties can request and be forced to produce thousands of pages of documents. Lawyers fly around the country taking depositions that seem to go on forever. The costs can be astronomical. Almost every client in every case complains at some point about the time, expense, and burden of discovery. There are a number of reasons for it.

Discovery can be used as a weapon. When the parties have unequal resources, the big guy can use discovery to grind down the little guy. The prospect of massive discovery can be powerful incentive to settle.

Discovery is also driven by gamesmanship. It's an understatement that litigators tend to be very competitive. Because of the adversarial nature of the process, those who aren't driven to win usually find another job. The gamesmanship in discovery manifests itself in many ways, from making and negotiating over frivolous objections to pushing lawyers and witnesses around in depositions. Some lawyers view discovery as an opportunity to demonstrate how aggressive, strong, or tough they are. Others consider it a chance to show off in front of their clients. The more discovery becomes a competition between lawyers or clients, the more it becomes wasteful.

Discovery can also become a habit. Many lawyers as a matter of course ask for every document and depose every witness. Others want excessive discovery because they fear not knowing everything before trial or being second-guessed for not taking a deposition. Lawyers may be uncomfortable evaluating the relative advantage of taking the deposition of a nonparty witness. They may not want to do a cost-benefit analysis which balances the expense of a deposition with the risk of the unknown.

Finally, billing structures may be a factor in the amount of discovery. Under an hourly billing arrangement, the lawyer makes most of his money in discovery. He has no incentive to do anything less than the most thorough and complete job. On the other hand, a lawyer working under a contingent fee arrangement has an incentive to minimize discovery. Because of these incentives, discovery is one area where you need to be aggressive in making sure that you and your lawyer are working together to achieve your goals at a price you want to pay.

DEPOSITIONS: WARMING UP FOR TRIAL

11

Don Healy, a real estate investor and developer, bought a mortgage supposedly secured by 72 lots on Nantucket Island, Massachusetts. Don knew when he bought it from the bank that another mortgage was senior on a few of the lots, but he thought he had a first mortgage on the vast majority. He later found that others had first mortgages on all of the lots. Since his mortgage was protected by a title insurance policy, he filed a claim against the title insurance company to recover the value of the lots that were supposedly subject to his first mortgage. The insurance company refused to pay because Don knew in advance about the title defect. Don then sued the company for the value of the lots.

After the parties produced documents, the title company sent a notice to take Don's deposition. Don was the type of guy who would talk to anybody about anything. He couldn't keep quiet. Moreover, since he didn't listen well, he tended to ramble on about whatever he wanted. He could not give precise answers to specific questions. He was nervous about his deposition because he didn't think he could control himself through two days of questioning by a hostile lawyer.

A deposition is the event at which you give live testimony before trial. Instead of testifying before a judge or jury, you appear in front of your opponent and his lawyer. Your opponent's lawyer can ask almost any question and you must answer under oath as if you were on trial. Because your answers under oath have the same effect as trial testimony and you are bound by them, your deposition can make or break your case. As you answer questions at your deposition, keep in mind your goals and how you will achieve them.

Your Goal at a Deposition

If you are a party to a case, your deposition will in most cases be for discovery. Your goal is to be as good a witness as possible in order to make your opponent nervous. You want to let him know how bad things can get at trial.

Demonstrating that you are a great witness does not mean that you want to tip your hand by volunteering information to educate your adversary. You typically want to give up as little as possible to limit your opponent's ability to undercut you in the courtroom. You want to employ the "rope-a-dope" strategy successfully used by Muhammad Ali in the "rumble in the jungle" fight with George Foreman. For five or six rounds, Ali stood on the ropes in a completely defensive position, with his forearms blocking his face and body. After Foreman punched himself out, Ali delivered the knockout punch, which you want to do at trial.

Your rope-a-dope strategy is to answer only the specific question asked. Your goal is not to present your best case. You cannot win a lawsuit in a deposition. You can only lose it. If, after your opponent is through, additional information should be disclosed, your lawyer can ask questions to permit you to say what you want.

How to Take a Deposition

The key to a successful deposition is to get the witness talking. Though lawyers differ on this point, the lawyer asking questions should begin in a calm, pleasant tone to ask open-ended questions designed to elicit long, narrative answers, not "yes" or "no" responses. For example, in Don's case, the title company's lawyer could have asked Don to describe what he knew about the other mortgages when he bought his or to explain everything the bank told him about the mortgage. These questions are far more effective than the leading, "yes" or "no" question: "Isn't it true that you knew about the title defects before you bought the mortgage?" By getting Don to talk, the lawyer maximizes his chances of getting information he doesn't know.

Once the dialogue has been established, the open-ended questions have been asked and the lawyer has elicited as much free information as he can, he can ask the specific, pointed, "yes" or "no" questions that pin a witness down. For example, after Don explains in general terms that he received some information about the title defects, the lawyer could ask Don the "yes" or "no" question: "Isn't it true that you knew about the title defects?"

For reasons that have never been clear to me, some lawyers launch into witnesses like mad dogs. They are loud and abrasive. They attempt to intimidate. They ask only "yes" or "no" questions. They often learn little in a deposition. They can also miss critical facts, only to be surprised at trial. In the end, they only increase hostility between the parties.

What Can You Ask About?

Your lawyer can ask about virtually anything in a deposition. The lawyer may ask about your education, your employment history, your family, or virtually anything else he can think of.

Many questions are a waste of time. However, some lawyers are in a rut. They ask the same questions in every case that painstakingly dig through irrelevant background information. Though every lawyer wants to start with some easy, non-controversial questions to get a witness talking, some go too far. However, there is nothing you can do about it, so be patient and stay as relaxed as you can.

Objections

Your lawyer will probably object to many questions in the deposition. Under the rules, objections are limited solely to the form of the question. Objectionable questions include those that are vague, ambiguous, unclear, or compound. For example, the compound question, "Isn't it true that you went to the store and then went to your friend's house and then went back home?" is objectionable because it seeks a "yes" or "no" answer but cannot be answered that way.

Objections other than to the form of the question are reserved until trial. Evidentiary objections such as hearsay or competence are raised when your opponent attempts to read the deposition to the jury. You are not supposed to make these objections during the deposition.

Notwithstanding this limitation, lawyers make long-winded objections on all sorts of issues. They do this to break the rhythm of the lawyer asking questions, give the client time to calm down or collect himself, cause the opposing lawyer to lose his train of thought, or generally obstruct the deposition. Good lawyers rarely use or fall for these tricks, which can be a basis for sanctions if too abusive. Though many clients like aggressive objections, it's best to play by the rules.

Preparing for a Deposition

Cases can be won or lost in a deposition. If you lock yourself into an untenable position, you may be unable to extricate yourself at trial. Because of its importance, you must prepare for your deposition in advance. Reacquaint yourself with the facts. Review important documents to refresh your recollection of what happened. Predict the questions your adversary will ask and decide how you will respond. Have your lawyer ask you questions so that you can practice your answers. Since a deposition is in effect your first day in court, you want to do it right.

You also want to get a good night's sleep before the deposition. Even seasoned deponents underestimate the energy needed to concentrate on questions and answers for a full day. Tired witnesses make mistakes. You don't want to say something that will come back to haunt you simply because you are weary.

How to Act at a Deposition

A deposition is in part a competition between you and your opponent's lawyer for control. Each of you seeks to dictate the pace and rhythm of the Q and A, and to disrupt the pace and rhythm of the other. You don't want your opponent's lawyer to steamroll you. You want the lawyer to know that when you are on the witness stand in court, you are in control and will be able to communicate your case credibly and persuasively. Consequently, consider the following tips:

Dictate the Timing

You can take as long as you want to answer a question. Don't rush. When your opponent's lawyer asks a question, think about it and then give a thoughtful, reasoned answer. If you hurry, you may make a mistake. Moreover, you may allow your opponent's lawyer to get in a rhythm. Lawyers like to ask a number of rapid-fire "yes" and "no" questions. After the witness gets in the habit of answering the questions, "yes, yes, yes, yes," the lawyer slips in a "no" question. However, the witness on a roll mistakenly answers the question "yes." If you take your time and control the rhythm yourself, this will not happen.

Moreover, you should pause long enough to allow your lawyer to object. If you don't leave some space between the end of the question and the start of your answer, your lawyer can't slip in the objection and the opportunity will be lost.

Listen to the Question

Many people don't listen well. This is a source of real trouble in depositions. If you don't fully understand what you're being asked, there is a very good chance that you will give the wrong answer. If you don't hear or understand a question, ask to hear it again. Don't answer an ambiguous question that could be used against you in the future.

Wait for the Entire Question

Listen not to a part but to the whole question. Some witnesses answer before the question is finished. As a result, they may answer a question that is different from the one the lawyer intends to ask. Even if they answer the right question, the court reporter cannot record a simultaneous question and answer and the transcript may not be clear.

Answer Only the Question Asked

The number one rule for any deposition is to answer only the question that's asked. Every witness breaks this rule many times during every deposition. For example, a common first question in a deposition is "Can you tell me your name?" The correct response to this question is "yes." Most witnesses respond by giving their names.

Witnesses routinely answer questions that are not asked for a number of reasons. First, depositions are stressful. Most

"I don't know" versus "I don't recall"

"I don't know" means that you never knew the answer to the question. "I don't recall" means that you may have once known, but don't remember at the deposition. "I don't recall" gives you more wiggle room for trial.

witnesses want to get them over as soon as possible. They mistakenly believe that by answering a question that should have been asked—not the question that was asked—they will finish sooner. They forget that a lawyer who asks the wrong question will not necessarily ask the right question, or that their unsolicited answer may lead to many more questions.

A lawyer taking a deposition of an expert witness in a water pollution case asked with great flourish, "Isn't it true that you have no evidence—absolutely no evidence—that the substance affects biological *orgasms*?" Though most of us would reply, "Don't you mean *organisms*?" the correct response is "yes." Additionally, though a deposition is adversarial, most witnesses want to be helpful. They answer the question that should have been asked because they want to provide information. These "free-will" offerings do nothing more than give your opponent information to use against you. They violate the rope-a-dope principle that governs depositions.

Be Succinct

Some witnesses like to talk. They give long, rambling answers to short, specific questions. If a question can be answered "yes" or "no," answer "yes" or "no." Don't give a five-minute monologue. In addition to giving your opponent free information that may hurt your case, each answer may provoke additional questions. A long answer generates many more questions than a short one. The best way to keep a deposition short is to keep your answers short.

Be Precise

In court, the only remnant of your deposition is a written transcript. Your emotion, inflection, and body language are lost. Since the only thing left is the cold, hard word, you want your words to be precise and clear.

Be Formal

You should be formal and professional in the deposition. In addition to the fact that colloquialisms can be ambiguous, you don't want to get into a dialogue with your opponent's lawyer. The lawyer hopes that the two of you will chat with each other as if you are chewing the fat in a local bar. He wants you to forget where you are and why you are there. You want to be as reserved as possible. Your opponent's lawyer is not your friend.

Read Documents Carefully

You will be asked questions about documents you produce in discovery. The lawyer may ask the definition of terms, the meaning of particular statements, the circumstances under which a document was written, or why a document was sent to someone.

Before you answer, read a document in its entirety. In some cases, you can understand certain paragraphs only by reading all paragraphs. Context may be essential. Watch out for a favorite lawyer trick—focusing a witness on a particular sentence in a document and getting him to interpret it in a way which, in the context of the entire document, does not make sense.

Moreover, by reading the entire document, you disrupt your opponent's pace. You assert control over the flow of the deposition, which always works to your benefit.

Don't Speculate

Many witnesses do not appreciate the difference between what they think and what they know. In a deposition, your duty is to tell what you know. You have no duty to speculate.

Speculation is a source of great trouble for witnesses. A lawyer often presents a witness with a reasonable, logical assumption that may be completely wrong. Witnesses, out of a desire to be helpful and appear knowledgeable, may adopt this assumption because it makes sense, even though they have no idea whether it is correct. There is nothing wrong with saying you don't know. Indeed, "I don't know" is one of the safest answers you can give at a deposition.

Deposition Checklist

☐ Prepare for the deposition.

☐ Read important documents in advance.

☐ Rehearse answers to anticipated questions.

☐ Listen to the question.

☐ Wait for the entire question.

☐ Think about your answer.

☐ Give your lawyer time to object.

☐ Answer only the question asked.

☐ Don't give information that's not requested.

☐ Set your own pace.

☐ Be succinct.

☐ Be precise.

☐ Don't use slang.

☐ Don't speculate.

☐ Read documents carefully.

☐ Admit what you don't know.

☐ Admit bad facts.

☐ Correct your mistakes.

☐ Keep cool.

☐ Don't fight with the opposing lawyer.

☐ Use the "rope-a-dope" method.

☐ Eat.

☐ Sleep.

☐ Tell the truth.

Speculation can create anxiety for witnesses. Once you start down the road, one speculation can lead to another. Before you know it, you are out on a limb. You may begin to wonder if you know what you're talking about. You may even question whether your speculations can be interpreted as false testimony. Stress rises because you don't know how to dig yourself out of the mess.

Tell the Truth

Always tell the truth at a deposition. In addition to the fact that you testify under oath and penalty of perjury and could go to jail if you lie, witnesses who tell the truth are good witnesses. It is very hard to weave a tangled web. Most witnesses who speculate, fudge, or downright lie do not appear credible. The truth is a safe place to be.

Admit Bad Facts

If your opponent's lawyer asks a point-blank question that doesn't help your case, admit it. Don't say you don't know if you do. Don't try to dodge the question with an evasive answer. Tell it like it is. It will give you credibility.

Correct a Mistake

If you make a mistake in your testimony and discover it before the end of the deposition, correct it immediately. It's better to admit the mistake at the deposition than at trial months later in front of the jury.

Many witnesses are afraid to admit mistakes. However, jurors know that people make mistakes all the time. If you make a mistake, simply say so and move on. Don't worry about it.

Keep Cool

Your opponent's lawyer may try to irritate or intimidate you. Don't let the lawyer bait you. Angry witnesses make mistakes. If you're being harassed, your lawyer should object. Let your lawyer fight with your adversary. Stay above the fray.

Listen to Objections

If your lawyer makes an objection that is something other than "objection to form," listen to it. He may be trying to send you a message.

Talking with Your Lawyer

You are not supposed to discuss questions and answers with your lawyer in the middle of a deposition. If your opponent asks a question that makes you nervous, you can't discuss your answer with your lawyer before you give it. You've got to answer on your own.

Confidential and Privileged Information

One exception to the rule that you can't talk to your lawyer about a pending question is when you are concerned about disclosing privileged communications or confidential business information. If you believe your answer falls into either of these categories, tell your lawyer and take a break to discuss whether and to what extent you must disclose the information.

Breaks

You can take a break any time you want, provided that no question is pending. Simply announce that you want one. If your opponent is on a roll, he may object, but there's nothing he can do about it.

Though you can take a break at any time, consider the message it sends to your adversary. If your opponent is bearing down on a sensitive area, your request for a break may communicate that your opponent has found a soft spot. Accordingly, don't take breaks under circumstances that communicate that you are nervous.

EVIDENCE: THE SCRIPT FOR THE PLAY

The police arrested Augie Maldanado for robbing a convenience store. Roger, the store attendant, would testify that Augie robbed him at gunpoint. Roger's girlfriend, Alice, was on the phone when she heard Augie tell Roger to empty the cash register or he'd "blow his brains out." The prosecution also had a videotape of Augie robbing Roger from a camera mounted behind the cash register. Finally, the police found Augie's .44 Magnum in the dumpster behind the store. All of this evidence would put Augie behind bars.

Evidence is the information you present in court to prove your claim. It includes oral testimony from witnesses, documents, videotapes and pictures the jury can see, physical evidence such as Augie's gun, and all other information the jury can consider in making a decision.

Because of the goal of ensuring that each side has a full and fair opportunity to present its act in the litigation play, rules of evidence limit the information the jury can review. These rules attempt to ensure that the jury considers only reliable and appropriate facts. Though the rules are extensive and at times complicated, certain issues come up in many cases.

Evidence Must Be Relevant

The prosecutor attempted to introduce evidence that Alice was so distraught by Augie's threat that she had a nervous breakdown. He argued that Alice's breakdown showed that Augie's threat was so violent that it proved that Augie would kill Roger if Roger didn't hand over the money. Augie objected because the evidence was not relevant to whether he robbed the store. He argued that its sole purpose was to make the jury mad at him, thereby increasing his chances of going to jail.

A jury should consider only evidence that tends to prove a consequential fact that will affect its decision one way or the other. However, relevant evidence can be excluded if it is unfairly prejudicial, confusing, misleading, cumulative, or a waste of time. Judges decide to exclude relevant evidence at their complete discretion. Accordingly, they can allow the jury to hear evidence you consider inappropriate, and there is very little you can do about it. Particularly in a civil case, where judges tend to be less concerned about prejudicial evidence, many judges allow the parties to present almost any evidence they want.

In Augie's case, though extremely prejudicial, evidence that Augie threatened to blow Roger's brains out would be admissible because it proves the armed robbery accusation. However, Alice's nervous breakdown wouldn't add much to the prosecutor's case and could be inflammatory. Because its prejudicial effect might substantially outweigh its relevance to the issue of armed robbery, a judge could exclude it.

Some have difficulty balancing relevance with unfair prejudice. They think that all harmful evidence is unduly prejudicial. Conversely, they think that all helpful evidence which, by definition, is harmful to the opponent, is admissible. This biased reaction of "let in the good" and "keep out the bad" arises at some point in every client in every case.

In analyzing the unfair prejudice issue, keep in mind that most bad evidence is admissible. Your opponent shouldn't offer it if it doesn't help him and hurt you. Unfairly prejudicial evidence typically has a significant, negative, emotional impact on the jury and has little to do with the issues in the lawsuit. It is unfair only in relation to its importance to the case. For example, evidence that the defendant has a habit of stealing money may be admissible in a theft case because, though prejudicial, it relates to a key issue. That same evidence may not be admissible in a medical malpractice case because, though equally prejudicial, it is far less relevant.

The bottom line is that the judge will probably allow your opponent to try the case the way he wants and introduce any evidence he thinks is appropriate. Most judges allow the jury to decide what is relevant. Therefore, unless you have a strong prejudice argument and the evidence has little to do with the case, assume that the jury will hear it.

Settlement and Insurance Evidence

Settlement offers before trial cannot be used to prove that you think you may be liable. Similarly, evidence that you have insurance cannot be admitted to show that you think you have a risk you need to insure against. These rules promote the public policies in favor of settlement and insurance. However, if you have another purpose for introducing settlement offers or insurance, the evidence is admissible for that other purpose and the jury can consider it however it wants.

Witnesses Must Be Competent

A witness must be competent to testify. In other words, witnesses must have the ability to know the information about which they will speak. Accordingly, they must have the mental and physical capacity to perceive, remember, recall and testify. For this reason, a two-month-old baby is not competent.

One of my partners once deposed an infirm, elderly woman. After 10 or 15 questions, she looked up at my partner and firmly asked, "So, when do we eat?" Since few confuse a deposition with a dinner party, she probably lacked the competence to testify.

In addition to having the ability to testify, a witness must in fact perceive, remember and recall the facts. For example, except in certain circumstances, only a witness who was present can testify about an automobile accident. If the witness didn't see a collision, then she lacks the personal knowledge to describe it. In Augie's case, Roger could testify about the robbery because he saw everything. Alice, on the other hand, was not in the convenience store and can testify only about what she personally heard over the phone.

Witnesses Testify Under Oath

To be competent, a witness must give an oath that he will testify truthfully. This is why every witness is sworn in and promises "to tell the truth, the whole truth, and nothing but the truth so help you God." Moreover, the penalty of perjury makes it a crime to give false testimony. The oath and penalty of perjury ensure that testimony is sufficiently credible for the jury to consider in making its decision.

Expert Witnesses

One exception to the rule that a witness must have personal knowledge of the facts is for expert witnesses. Experts are allowed to give opinions about scientific, technical or other specialized topics when their testimony will help the jury understand the facts or decide the case. Any person with special knowledge, skill, experience, training, or education can be an expert witness.

Experts are an important part of many lawsuits. They testify about whether a building was properly constructed, a product was properly manufactured or a doctor or lawyer was negligent. They opine on the nature and severity of the injury of a slip-and-fall or automobile-accident victim. They state the value of a home or business. They project the amount of lost profits. Because they often opine on the key issues in a lawsuit, many cases are a battle of the experts.

In giving an opinion, an expert can rely on and explain to the jury evidence that is not otherwise admissible, provided that other experts reasonably rely upon this type of information in forming their opinions. Consequently, experts are often used to introduce substantial amounts of evidence that you can't get before the jury any other way. For example, if Alice sues Augie for causing her nervous breakdown, Alice's doctor could recount statements from Alice's many friends about her constant twitches and amnesia. Though the doctor's recitation of statements by others would be hearsay, if doctors usually rely on these kinds of statements, they would be admissible for the purpose of supporting the doctor's opinion. By using a doctor to present the out-of-court statements, you avoid calling additional witnesses and put a professional gloss to the evidence.

Character Evidence

Generally speaking, character evidence is not admissible. You can't simply disparage your opponent in the hope that the jury will dislike him and rule in your favor. This rule is difficult for aggressive litigants who want to introduce as much dirt as possible to attack their opponents.

Character evidence can be used for impeachment. Impeachment is the term for attacking or undermining the credibility of a witness, regardless of whether the witness is a party to the suit. For example, questions designed to cause the jury to conclude that a witness doesn't remember or is lying are impeachment questions.

Opinions or testimony about a witness's reputation for failing to tell the truth can be used for impeachment. For example, if a witness has a reputation around town for being a liar, then members of the community who know that reputation can testify to it. Once someone testifies that the witness has a reputation as a liar, others can testify that the impeached witness has a reputation for truthfulness. Except in certain circumstances, testimony about specific conduct—that on July 24, the witness lied to me about a stolen car, for example—cannot be introduced. Rather, this kind of testimony is limited to opinion and reputation.

Evidence Must Be Authentic

Documents, photographs, videotapes, and other tangible evidence must be authentic to be admissible. You must prove that the evidence is what you claim it is. For example, to prove Cathy Crabtree wrote a letter, a witness could identify Cathy's handwriting. To authenticate a contract, a witness could verify the signatures of the people who signed it. For tape recordings, a witness familiar with the speaker's voice should state that the speaker is on the tape. For the convenience store videotape, Roger could establish that it depicts what happened in the store at the time of the robbery. The principle underlying each of these examples is the same. You must show that your evidence is what you claim it is and, therefore, is reliable.

Privileged Information

In preparing for trial, Augie told his lawyer that he robbed the store with the gun the police found in the dumpster. Though others could be subpoenaed to testify to what Augie told them, the lawyer could not. This is because statements from Augie to his lawyer are privileged.

You are not required to disclose communications made in privileged relationships, such as attorney-client, doctor-patient, minister-parishioner, and husband-wife. The purpose of the privileges is to allow you to communicate freely and confidentially within these relationships. For example, the doctor-patient privilege ensures that the physician receives complete information in order to provide treatment. The attorney-client privilege ensures that the lawyer has all of the facts necessary to render legal advice. Though each privilege is a little bit different, a few basic principles apply to all:

Privileges Apply to Communications

Privileges apply only to communications between the parties in the relationship. These include oral statements, written memoranda, sign language, two winks of the eye, or any other means of transmitting information. If you're not dealing with a communication, then a privilege can't apply.

The Communication Must Be Confidential

To be privileged, the communication cannot be disclosed to a third party. Accordingly, if you want to have a privileged conversation with your lawyer or doctor, make sure nobody else is around.

You Must Intend That the Communication Be Privileged

You must also communicate under circumstances which demonstrate that you expect that the communication will remain confidential. You can't, for example, carry on a loud, privileged conversation with your lawyer at a cocktail party. Even though no one may hear what you say because of the racket, a dialogue in a crowded room does not suggest that you intend that the communication to be confidential.

The Communication Must Be for a Privileged Purpose

For a conversation with your lawyer to be privileged, you must communicate for the purpose of getting legal advice. If you talk to your doctor, the information must be necessary for diagnosis and treatment in order for the communication to be privileged. If the communication is not for the purpose to which the privilege relates, it is not privileged.

The Recipient Must Be Acting in a Privileged Capacity

If you talk with your lawyer about stock tips or basketball scores, the privilege does not apply because he is not acting in the role of a lawyer in the conversation.

The Fifth Amendment Privilege

In addition to privileges which arise out of various relationships, the U.S. Constitution includes a privilege against self-incrimination. As you may recall from TV shows, "You have the right to remain silent, and anything you say can and will be used against you." Under this privilege, you do not have to say anything that might tend to incriminate you. However, the absolute right not to speak relates only to criminal activity—where there is a real risk of incrimination. It does not apply to immoral or embarrassing conduct.

Under this privilege, Augie could not be forced to testify at his criminal trial. Like O. J. Simpson, he could simply rely on other witnesses to provide his defense. However, also like O. J. Simpson, Augie could be forced to testify in Alice's civil case because once the criminal trial is over, he no longer has a risk of incrimination and the privilege no longer exists.

Only the Owner of the Privilege Can Assert It

Only the client or patient can assert a privilege. The doctor or lawyer has no right to claim that a communication is privileged. Rather, the lawyer or doctor must follow the instructions of the client to protect a privileged communication.

Waiver of the Privilege

Only the person who owns the privilege can waive it. Consequently, neither your lawyer, your doctor, or anyone else is

Privileged Communications

To be privileged, you must have a communication . . .

1. That is confidential.

2. That you intend to be confidential.

3. That is made for a privileged purpose.

4. That is received for a privileged purpose.

5. That hasn't been waived.

authorized to disclose without your prior authorization any information you communicate in confidence.

One risk with privileged communications is that they are all or nothing. If you waive the privilege in one instance, you waive it in all instances. If you disclose privileged information to your friend, you lose the right to keep it from your enemy. Similarly, if you have a slip of the tongue and disclose only a small piece of privileged information, you may "open the door" and be required to disclose all related privileged information. Consequently, you should be vigilant in protecting yourself against disclosure of privileged communications.

Hearsay

Hearsay is a statement made out of court which is recounted in court for the purpose of proving the truth of the fact asserted in the out-of-court statement. For example, testimony in court by Peter Rabbit that Chicken Little told him that "the sky is falling" is hearsay if offered to prove that the sky was in fact falling. The out-of-court statement is Chicken Little's exclamation that Peter recounts in court. The purpose of the evidence—to prove that the sky was falling—is to prove the truth of the fact asserted in Chicken Little's exclamation.

Note that Peter Rabbit's statement would not be hearsay if offered to prove that Chicken Little is crazy. It would not be offered to prove the truth that's asserted—that the sky is falling. For this reason, lawyers often try to introduce hearsay statements into evidence for some other purpose. Since a jury generally considers evidence for more than one limited purpose, lawyers try to get hearsay statements into evidence any way they can. They hope that evidence introduced for one purpose will be considered for all purposes.

The hearsay rule applies not only to oral statements. It also applies to any assertion, including nonverbal conduct, provided the assertion is a communication. Thus, any statement in whatever form may be subject to the hearsay rule.

As with other rules, the purpose of the hearsay rule is to exclude unreliable evidence. Hearsay is inadmissible because the speaker is not in court subject to the test of cross-examination. Since all in-court statements are subject to cross-examination, hearsay is sufficiently less reliable than court testimony.

There are numerous exceptions to the rule which are not considered hearsay either by definition or because they are expressly excepted. The circumstances surrounding these out-of-court statements cause them to be sufficiently reliable and admissible. The most commonly used exceptions are as follows:

Prior Inconsistent Statements

When the witness makes a statement under oath in a prior deposition, trial, or other proceeding which is inconsistent with the current court testimony, then the prior testimony is not hearsay. For example, if Alice testified in Augie's criminal trial that she heard nothing over the phone, that statement would not be hearsay in Alice's subsequent civil case against Augie when she testified that she heard Augie threaten to shoot Roger. The prior contradictory statement is reliable because it was made under oath and penalty of perjury.

Prior Consistent Statements

A prior statement that is consistent with the current testimony is not hearsay if offered to rebut a claim that the witness recently made up the current testimony. For example, if Augie claimed in Alice's civil trial that Alice recently made up her story that she heard Augie threaten to shoot Roger, then Alice could introduce prior statements to the police about Augie's threat. Consistency with testimony under oath makes these statements reliable.

Admissions by Your Opponent

A statement by your opponent that hurts her case is not hearsay on the assumption that people won't admit something negative about their own case unless it's true. For example, if Augie admitted to the police that he threatened to blow Roger's brains out, the police officer could testify to Augie's admission in Alice's civil trial.

Present Sense Impressions

A description of an event occurring contemporaneously with the statement is not hearsay. For example, Chicken Little's statement that the sky is falling might come within this exception in that Chicken Little is describing the falling sky while watching it. A communication about a contemporaneous event is reliable because there is no time lapse to give the speaker time to falsify his statement or to affect his ability to remember, recall, and recount.

Excited Utterances

An excited utterance is also not hearsay. This would, for example, include a scream by a customer in Roger's convenience store that Augie has "got a gun." This statement is much like a present sense impression in that both rely on spontaneity for reliability. In most cases, either exception applies.

State of Mind

A witness's statement about his existing state of mind, emotion, sensation or physical condition, including intent, plan, motive, design, mental feeling, pain, or bodily health, is not hearsay. For example, Alice's statement to her mother that she "is afraid for Roger's life" is not hearsay because it describes Alice's mental and emotional condition—fear. Since this exception relates to an existing state of mind, it too relies on contemporaneousness for reliability.

Hearsay

Hearsay is an out-of-court statement . . .

- ◆ To prove the truth of the fact asserted.
- ◆ That's not inconsistent with a prior statement.
- ◆ That's not a negative admission.
- ◆ That doesn't describe a state of mind.
- ◆ That's not a contemporaneous report.
- ◆ That's not a business record.

Medical Diagnosis or Treatment

Statements made for the purpose of medical diagnosis or treatment or describing medical conditions or history are not hearsay. These statements are deemed reliable on the assumption that you won't lie to your doctor if you need help.

Business Records

Many kinds of records kept in the ordinary course of business are not hearsay. These records are reliable because they are regularly kept and checked according to a business system. Similarly, the absence of records of an event that would be recorded in the ordinary course of business is admissible to prove that an event did not occur.

Other Reliable Statements

In addition to other exceptions, there is a final catch-all that allows the court to admit any hearsay evidence that is sufficiently trustworthy and not unduly prejudicial. Though different judges react to this exception in different ways, you always have a chance to get hearsay into evidence.

THE STANDARD OF LIABILITY: THE BURDEN OF PROOF **13**

Many believe that the jury correctly held that O.J. Simpson was "not guilty" in his criminal trial. They also believe that O.J. murdered Nicole Brown and Ronald Goldman and should have been liable for millions of dollars in damages in the civil case filed by their families. The reason O.J. Simpson is "not guilty" but also "liable" is the burden of proof.

The burden of proof is the standard by which a jury judges disputed facts. In a traffic case, a plaintiff who is smashed into an intersection claims that the defendant ran a red light. Not surprisingly, the defendant claims the traffic light was green. The jury must decide whether the light was red or green. It uses the burden of proof to weigh the conflicting evidence.

The government in a criminal case or the plaintiff in a civil case presents evidence which it believes is sufficient to satisfy the burden of proof. If the government or plaintiff convinces the jury that it meets the standard, then it wins. If it does not, then the defendant wins.

Different burdens of proof apply depending upon the claims in the case and the stage in the lawsuit. Some burdens are familiar, such as "beyond a reasonable doubt" and "probable cause." Others are less well known, such as "preponderance of evidence." Each standard governs whether the plaintiff or the government has the right to continue a case or ultimately win at trial.

Criminal Burdens of Proof

There are two principal burdens of proof in criminal law. A criminal case can begin when a judge or grand jury finds that there is "probable cause" that the defendant committed a crime. Probable cause exists if a hypothetical reasonable person would believe that the defendant committed the crime. If the government cannot convince a judge or grand jury that a reasonable person would believe this, then it cannot start a criminal proceeding.

Even if a defendant is charged with a crime based on probable cause, he is presumed innocent until proven guilty at trial. At trial, the government attempts to prove beyond a reasonable doubt that the defendant committed the crime. "Beyond a reasonable doubt" is higher than "probable cause" because the hypothetical reasonable person must believe that the only reasonable conclusion is that the defendant committed a crime. Once a criminal case reaches trial, the focus of the case shifts from whether a crime is one reasonable explanation to whether it is the only reasonable explanation for what happened. If the government does not prove that the defendant committed the crime beyond a reasonable doubt, then the jury should not convict him. Moreover, if the government does not present enough evidence to cause the judge to believe that a reasonable person could convict the defendant, then the judge should summarily dismiss the case without allowing the jury to even consider whether the defendant is guilty. Under the red/green light analogy, the case shifts from proof that the defendant may have run a red light to proof that the only reasonable explanation for the collision is that the light was red.

In the O.J. Simpson criminal case, the prosecution claimed that the only reasonable explanation for the deaths of Brown and Goldman was that O.J. killed them. The defense suggested other scenarios, including more than one killer and a drug hit. In finding O.J. "not guilty," the jury apparently concluded that at least one of these alternative scenarios was reasonable. Consequently, they did not find O.J. guilty beyond a reasonable doubt.

"In America, an acquittal doesn't mean you're innocent. It means you beat the wrap. My clients lose even when they win."

—F. Lee Bailey

Not guilty is different from "innocent." "Not guilty" means only that the government failed to meet the burden of proof. For example, the fact that the jury found O.J. Simpson not guilty does not mean that it did not believe that he killed Brown and Goldman. The jury did not and could not find O.J. innocent because its only job was to decide whether he was guilty beyond a reasonable doubt. Moreover, the fact that the jury found O.J. not guilty of the criminal charge says nothing about whether he should be liable by a preponderance of the evidence in the civil case.

Burdens of Proof

- ◆ Preponderance of the evidence
- ◆ Clear and convincing evidence
- ◆ Beyond a reasonable doubt

The burden of proof in a civil suit is lower than in a criminal case. However, the burden for beginning a civil lawsuit is very similar to the criminal standard. You should not file a complaint unless you have evidence to prove your case or you reasonably believe that you can find that evidence. Moreover, your claims should be valid under the law. This standard is much like the "probable cause" standard in a criminal case.

At trial, you have the burden to prove your claims by a preponderance of the evidence, which means "more likely than not." Similarly, a defendant must prove his counterclaims under the same standard. This burden, which is just more than 50 percent, is greater than a reasonable belief that a claim exists under one of many factual scenarios, but far less than beyond a reasonable doubt. It means tipping the scales of justice ever so slightly in your favor. If the claims involve fraud, you may have to meet the higher burden of "clear and convincing proof."

The Burden of Proof Makes a Difference

Differences in the burden of proof affect strategies and tactics in trials. In a criminal case, the defendant does not have to prove that he is right and the government is wrong. He does not have to say where he was or what he was doing when the crime was committed. He only needs to show that there is one reasonable version of the facts under which he did not commit the crime. For this reason, O.J. Simpson never told the jury what he was doing on the night of the Brown and Goldman murders. He had no need to answer the jury's questions in order to be found "not guilty." He created a reasonable doubt by suggesting through other evidence that there was at least one reasonable alternative scenario.

In a civil case, each side has a 50/50 chance of winning. The case is a toss-up. A defendant must tell his side of the story. He must prove that he is right and the plaintiff is wrong. If not, he will probably lose the case. In the trial of the civil case, O.J. Simpson had to say where he was and what he was doing at the time of the murders. In order to win, he had to prove that he is not a murderer. Because he did not, he was found liable for millions of dollars in damages.

Because of the different burdens of proof, it is easier for a plaintiff to prove that a defendant owes him money than it is for the government to convict a defendant of a crime and send him to jail. We force a defendant to pay money yet allow him to stay out of jail because we have decided that the government should not deprive a citizen of his liberty unless a group of ordinary citizens, a jury of peers, is unanimously certain beyond a reasonable doubt that he is guilty of a crime. We err on the side of allowing a guilty person to go free rather than risk putting an innocent person in jail.

> "It is better to risk saving a guilty man than to condemn an innocent one."
>
> —Voltaire

In a civil case, the issue is money, not the loss of liberty. The more extreme penalty of imprisonment is not an option. A civil case also involves a dispute between two equal citizens, not an attempt by society to punish someone. For these reasons, we use the preponderance of the evidence burden of proof, which establishes a level playing field for both parties. We have decided that when a dispute is between two citizens, each should have an equal shot at winning.

SETTLEMENT: GETTING OUT 14

Bill Armstrong, an engineer for a large equipment manufacturer, was fired when he was 56 years old. He was so angry that he was replaced by a 37-year-old that he filed an age discrimination lawsuit. He rejected a settlement offer of $65,000 early in the case. After a trial four years later, he collected $74,000. By that time, his anger had subsided and he had moved on with his life. He regretted that he did not take $65,000 early in the case.

You should keep the prospect of settlement in mind throughout the course of a lawsuit. Do not forget that the sole purpose of a lawsuit is to resolve the dispute at terms that are acceptable to you. Parties often forget this fact as they become involved in the litigation, and winning the lawsuit becomes a goal in and of itself.

Because litigation is inefficient, expensive, and time-consuming, you should frequently evaluate the settlement value of your case. You should do a new, independent analysis each time a significant event occurs. If you learn new facts that help or hurt you, or the judge enters a ruling that is good or bad, reevaluate your case.

You may also want to reconsider settlement whenever your personal circumstances change. For example, if you are a plaintiff, you may be more anxious to settle today than a year ago because you need the cash more now than you did before.

A lawsuit should be evaluated based on the particular facts and circumstances that exist on the date of analysis without regard to your prior opinions of the value of the case. As with buying, selling, or holding stock, every day is a new day in evaluating whether to continue litigation or settle. Consequently, you should constantly consider how to evaluate the case, when to settle, how to settle, and for how much.

How to Evaluate Your Case

A good way to evaluate a case for settlement is to make lists. One list should include all of the claims in the case. For each of these claims, list the important factual and legal issues that are likely to affect the jury's decision. The list should highlight both strengths and weaknesses. As with your initial evaluation of the case, be mindful of the principle of selective perception and the tendency to put too much weight on your strengths and your opponent's weaknesses and not enough emphasis on your weaknesses and your opponent's strengths. Regardless of how right you think you are, your opponent probably feels that he is also right. The truth for the jury is often somewhere in the middle.

Once you make your lists, figure out your chances of winning and losing each of the claims. Many find it helpful to assign probabilities to the jury's possible conclusions on each claim. For example, City Cab sued Acme Auto Repair for breach of contract and fraud. City Cab claimed that Acme Auto failed to repair cabs as agreed and also misrepresented some of the work it promised to do. In evaluating the settlement, City Cab listed all of the factual and legal strengths and weaknesses of the claims. It concluded that it had a 70 percent chance of winning the breach of contract claim, but only a 30 percent chance of winning the fraud claim. These probabilities formed the basis of its settlement analysis.

After evaluating your chances of winning and losing each claim, predict the likely remedies. In a typical case, the jury will award money damages. In some cases, damages cannot be projected with precision, and you must consider a range of possible damages awards. However, you should predict to the extent possible the probability of winning or losing a specific amount of money. Moreover, since the bottom-line issue is the amount of dollars that will end up in your pocket, you should also deduct your costs of litigation. Consequently, you should net out your projected legal fees and other expenses of getting through the trial.

For example, City Cab predicted that damages on the fraud claim ranged from $125,000 to $325,000. It assumed that the cost of litigating the case through trial was $25,000. Thus, it concluded that the likely damages award, net of expenses, ranged from $100,000 to $300,000. Since City Cab assumed that either end of the range was equally possible, it projected $200,000. Since it predicted a 30 percent chance of winning the fraud claim, it concluded that the settlement value was in the $60,000 range.

Many lawyers dislike this type of analysis. They refuse to give percentages. They say that litigation is too unpredictable because "juries can do anything." If your lawyer refuses to be pinned down, push him. It's too easy for him to say you have "a pretty good claim" or an "okay case." Moreover, vagueness doesn't help you in evaluating the settlement value of your case. Experienced lawyers know what a case is worth. Demand specific probabilities of winning or losing.

This probability analysis is purely economic. It ignores many factors that may be difficult to quantify but should be factored into the settlement mix. Keep the larger picture in mind. Focus not just on obtaining the best economic result from a jury, but also on achieving your underlying goals. For example, in addition to recovering the maximum amount possible from Acme Auto, City Cab may also want to avoid the time, expense, and distraction of the lawsuit. It may not want its managers, drivers, and maintenance workers drawn away from the taxi business to work on the litigation. Litigation can also be a significant emotional drain on all who are touched by it. Though difficult to measure, City Cab may value avoiding litigation, which could cause it to accept a lesser settlement.

> "To be a trial lawyer is to see the ignominy of slow justice in a system in which the process itself punishes all who come in contact with it—the winner as well as the loser."
>
> —John A. Jenkins

A second factor is the extent to which you are willing to assume risks. A pure probability analysis doesn't always take into account the old adage that "a bird in the hand is worth two in the bush." For example, City Cab might accept $40,000 in settlement because trials are inherently unpredictable, and it would rather have $40,000 in the bank in exchange for avoiding the risk of recovering zero, even though a pure probability analysis suggests that the fraud claim is worth $60,000. You may also want to factor in the time value of money. Depending on interest rates, money today may be worth far more than money in three years after the trial. Unless prejudgment interest is accruing on your claim, which may or may not happen on the type of claim and applicable law, you may want to take less in exchange for getting the money sooner rather than later.

In determining the settlement value of a case, be objective. Your emotions will affect you. Your sense of right and wrong will color your analysis. Jurors, however, do not walk into the case with the same sense of righteous indignation. Since in evaluating a case for settlement you are trying to look through the eyes of jurors, not your own, you must put aside your feelings.

Moreover, consider the impact of your prior expectations on your settlement analysis. When parties assume a reasonable settlement value, they may become wedded to that value and reluctant to budge off the "number," even though new facts and circumstances suggest that the value has changed. Since the value often diminishes as the parties learn more about their adversary's strengths and their own weaknesses, and the enthusiasm for litigation wanes, litigants may become stuck on a settlement number which is simply too high and expect too much in settlement.

Under the principle of loss aversion, we are less able to accept a reduced settlement value because, from a psychological standpoint, we do not want to "give up" what we expect. Conversely, we tend to be more objective in evaluating settlements that are above our "number" because we are receiving what is in effect found money. We don't feel like we are giving up money we have psychologically put in the bank. Obviously, these tendencies should be resisted. A case should be evaluated with the same objective view regardless of where the proposed settlement amount is in relation to prior expectations.

Who Settles the Case?

The client and only the client is ultimately responsible for settling a case. You should receive counsel, advice, and even pressure from others. However, only you should make the settlement decision.

The lawyer's role in the settlement process is to provide advice, not to make decisions. The lawyer should describe what he thinks will happen in the case, review the factual and legal strengths and weaknesses, explain possible outcomes, and assign probabilities to the likelihood of particular outcomes. This is critical input for the client in making the settlement decision. However, the buck should stop with the client.

In many instances, clients look to their lawyers to tell them what to do. This is natural in that the lawyer is viewed as "the expert," and the decision of when to settle and for how much is often difficult. Though many clients ask their lawyers to make these decisions for them, you should remember that the lawyer's interests may be different from yours.

Lawyers handle lawsuits on behalf of their clients because it is their job. Though most lawyers want their clients to go away happy, once the litigation is over, the client and the case are often forgotten and the lawyer moves on to the next case. While lawyers want to get the best possible result for their clients, they also want to enhance their own professional life and ensure that they work on cases that are fun and profitable. For this reason, lawyers have an unavoidable tendency to promote settlement to get rid of cases or clients they don't like or are not profitable. Conversely, they are not saddened by big-fee–generating cases that don't settle. As a judge once said to the lawyers in a case that didn't settle: "You guys are going to put your kids through college on this one." When looking at settlement options, examine the case from your own personal point of view, and filter out any influence that may arise out of the conflicting interests of your lawyer.

The conflict in interest between lawyer and client can be particularly true in contingent-fee cases. When the lawyer is paid a percentage of the recovery, the lawyer's incentive is to get the biggest fee for the smallest amount of work. If the lawyer receives one-third of any recovery, settling a case for $100,000 after two weeks of work may be much better for the lawyer than settling the case for $200,000 in the middle of trial, three years after filing the lawsuit and after running up $100,000 in legal fees on an hourly rate. The difference for the lawyer is $33,000 for very little work or $67,000 for $100,000 worth of work. The client, on the other hand, might prefer to recover $133,000 in three years rather than only $67,000 in two weeks.

Different conflicting interests arise when the same lawyer in the same case is paid on an hourly basis. Now his incentive is to settle the case in the middle of trial, after he has collected $100,000 in attorney's fees. The client, on the other hand, would receive the same amount regardless of whether he settles immediately for $100,000 or for $200,000 during trial after paying the lawyer $100,000 in fees.

Judges may also influence the settlement process. Many believe that they have a duty to get rid of cases before trial to reduce their workloads and allow other cases to move through the system more quickly. To facilitate settlement, many judges hold settlement conferences, which are meetings among the judge, the lawyers, and sometimes also the clients. The sole purpose of these conferences is to cause the parties to settle. However, do not assume that realistic settlement possibilities will be discussed.

Many judges hold settlement conferences without adequate preparation. They do not study the factual and legal strengths and weaknesses of a case, and they often are not able to give a realistic analysis. Some judges nevertheless state with great certainty and persuasion the weaknesses of your case, the strengths of your opponent's case, and the amount for which you should settle. Do not necessarily put much weight on what may be a judge's uninformed opinion. Moreover, recall that the judge does not represent you and is not motivated to ensure that you get a fair settlement. He may want to convince you to settle no matter what. In other words, don't necessarily trust what the judge says about your case.

Judges may hold settlement conferences with lawyers but not clients. The judge's goal in these conferences is to get the lawyers to agree on a settlement and then get them to convince their clients to go along with it. Since it is your case and you have the right to make all settlement decisions, you can object to this procedure. If you want to participate in the conference, tell your lawyer. There is no reason that you shouldn't be able to join in every aspect of the settlement process.

When Do You Settle?

You can settle a case at any time. You should settle a case as soon as you can, provided that you get a reasonable amount of money. There is no reason to drag out your lawsuit. As with Bill Armstrong, in many cases a client rejects a settlement offer early in a case which, in hindsight after years of litigation, he wishes he had taken.

Some say that making the first settlement offer is a sign of weakness. While that once may have been true, it's not true today. Many recognize that full-blown litigation is a waste of time and money and that any reasonable attempt to avoid that waste is

Case Evaluation

- ☐ What are the factual strengths and weaknesses?
- ☐ What are the legal strengths and weaknesses?
- ☐ What are the chances of winning and losing?
- ☐ What are the damages?
- ☐ What is the downside?
- ☐ How much will it cost to continue?
- ☐ How much time will you spend?
- ☐ How much energy will you spend?
- ☐ How much will it distract you?
- ☐ What is the emotional drain?
- ☐ Are you settling everything?
- ☐ Are there any loose ends?
- ☐ Are you being objective?
- ☐ Are you making the decision?
- ☐ Are there better alternatives to settlement?

productive. Accordingly, don't be shy about making the first settlement offer.

However, if your settlement proposal is refused, you may not want to make another one until the time is right. Proposing a second settlement option after the first has been flatly rejected may be a sign of weakness. Lawyers call this "bidding against yourself." If you've made an offer that has been rejected, don't make another one until the circumstances in the case change and your adversary perceives that it is a new settlement day.

In considering when to make a settlement offer, the best time is usually when the risk and uncertainty for your adversary are greatest. Risk and uncertainty create insecurity, which is an emotion that settlement discussions can exploit. For example, a good time to propose settlement may be after you file a motion for summary judgment. This motion is in effect a request that the judge throw out your opponent's case and declare you the winner. While the judge is considering your motion, the risk, uncertainty, and insecurity for your opponent may be greater than if the motion had not been filed at all. This is because with one stroke of the pen, the judge could end the case in your favor. By creating this risk and uncertainty in the mind of your adversary, you maximize your settlement leverage.

For How Much Should You Settle?

They say that on Wall Street there are "bulls, bears, and pigs." The same is true with litigation. When you're looking at settlement options, don't be a pig.

The chances are that at trial, the jury will give the plaintiff less than she asks for and less than she thinks she is entitled to get. Similarly, unless he wins outright, the defendant will probably pay more than he thinks he should. Both parties will probably pay more in legal fees and expenses than they project. Consequently, in most cases, by the time all is said and done, everybody will have less than they expect.

Parties to lawsuits also often underestimate the time and energy required to litigate a case through trial. They miscalculate the time away from other activities, the disruption in their daily lives, and the emotional drain of thinking about the case some or all of the time. They do not appreciate the fact that litigation can be a pain in the neck. These factors should also be considered when developing an appropriate settlement amount.

There is no precise formula to figuring out for how much you should settle. The only rule of thumb is that a plaintiff should probably settle for less than he wants and a defendant should pay something, even though he thinks he is 100 percent right. Do not ignore the old adage that a good settlement is one with which neither side is happy.

What Are You Settling?

In most cases, when the parties settle a lawsuit, they dismiss all claims and sign a release. A release is the document by which you surrender the claims you have against your opponent. Releases vary in scope. Consequently, when negotiating a settlement, ensure that the release dismisses the claims that have been resolved and preserves the rest.

The most typical form of release is a general release. It surrenders all claims. Through this release, you give up not only the claims in the case, but also all other claims, including claims you don't even know about. In this instance, be careful that you are not giving up more than you want.

A release can be limited to the extent that the parties agree. For example, the release can be limited solely to the claims alleged in the lawsuit. Sometimes the parties release only some of the claims and agree to preserve and resolve the remaining claims another day. Because the scope of releases varies, negotiation of the terms of the release can be a significant settlement issue.

When you review the settlement documents, read them closely to make sure that you fully understand the fine print. If you and your opponent don't have a meeting of the minds on the specific claims that are being settled and released, you could have more litigation down the road as to what was and wasn't released. Since a settlement is like the sale of a legal claim from the plaintiff to the defendant, and the value of the settlement is based primarily on the value of the claims sold and released, be sure you get what you bargained for.

PRETRIAL PREP: PRODUCING THE PLAY

Like any successful play, most of the work is done before the show starts. You should pay significant attention to the actors, script, costumes, props, set design, and rehearsal. A polished, organized production that effectively communicates your theme greatly enhances your chances of victory. An unfocused, disorganized, unclear presentation virtually guarantees a loss. Before you start the trial, think through everything that may happen and prepare to respond. Something unexpected always occurs, but you will be better able to deal with it if you have dotted all of your "i"s and crossed all of your "t"s before hand.

Define Your Theme

A key to succeeding at trial is to develop a clear, tight, short, plausible theme. If accepted, this theme should lead to the conclusion that you win and your opponent loses. Your theme must be supported by the evidence. If it is not, your theme will be rejected by the jury.

The best way to create a theme is to begin with the phrase, "This is a story about. . . ." If you can't finish the theme in two sentences, it is too long and complicated. You should have a simple explanation for your case.

> "[Preparation] is the be-all of good trial work. Everything else—felicity of expression, improvisational brilliance—is a satellite around the sun. Thorough preparation is that sun."
>
> —Lewis Nizer

Write the Script

If you don't start with a solid script, your play will not be a success. This script should emphasize the theme of your case. Evidence that makes up your story should support your theme or undercut your opponent's.

As you assemble your evidence, pay particular attention to the fact that juries and judges decide cases based not only on what they intellectually think is right, but also on what they emotionally feel is right. One judge I know admits that he first decides what is fair and just—what he feels is right—and then figures out a way to justify his decision based on the law and facts. If you win the heart of the judge or jury, the mind will usually follow.

> "The ethical distinction between lying to a jury and pulling the wool over its eyes is surely a fine one."
>
> —Phillip E. Johnson

The landscape of the case you paint for the jury should be more than an English countryside filled with horses and hounds jumping over hedgerows. Linear paintings of rural England do not generate emotions or inspire action, they fill space on your office wall. Your script should paint a Monet filled with color and emotion. Once the jury feels that you are right, it will draw inferences your way. It will see the glass half full if you want it to be half full, and half empty if you want it to be half empty. It will want you to win.

The best way to create the right impression is to tell a story the jury can identify with and relate to. This story should tap into basic notions of truth, justice, right, and wrong. If it provokes thoughts and feelings that jurors have felt in the past, and that they know are true, you are halfway to victory. On the other hand, if you simply present a dry history of events that does not touch the personal experiences of the jurors or the experiences of humans generally, you will not be convincing.

> "Law school taught me one thing: 'How to take two situations that are exactly the same and show how they are different.'"
>
> —Hart Pomerantz

Tom Ryan was the lawyer for a paint distributor whose franchise was terminated by its manufacturer. A key issue in the case was the manufacturer's control over the franchise. Under the contract, the franchisee had the legal right to set prices and inventory levels, hire and fire its own employees, and devise its own marketing plans. However, if it didn't comply with the manufacturer's requests, it could be terminated. Rather than focus on control by the manufacturer, Tom talked about a marriage between the manufacturer and the franchisee. Each of the manufacturer's witnesses admitted that though they had the absolute right to do what they wanted every Saturday and Sunday over their wives' objections, they wouldn't do so because they knew their marriages would end in divorce if they did. They also agreed their wives' right of divorce was a form of control over them, much like the manufacturer's right of termination over the franchisee. By emphasizing the marriage theme—that their wives' power was just like the manufacturer's power—Tom was better able to reach each juror's personal feelings and experiences.

The script should unfold clearly, simply, and naturally. Like any other good story, it should flow along a time line from beginning to end. Though on rare occasions you may want to present a case topically, most of us think and process information chronologically.

Unlike a Broadway show, you do not write out your script. You do not memorize questions and answers. Overly scripted plays appear stilted and contrived. They do not ring true. You want your story to appear to develop spontaneously before the jury. Accordingly, your script is largely a detailed list of the evidence you want to present in the order that you will present it.

You should review all of the facts in the case as you prepare the script. Read the deposition transcripts. Review all of the documents produced by each side in discovery. Talk with your witnesses. Define the universe of potential evidence before making decisions about what you will or won't use.

Plan your testimony. Outline the order in which you will present your evidence. Consider the areas you want to emphasize to support your theme. Identify the witnesses who will present particular facts. Determine whether there are any bad facts that will come out on cross-examination or through your opponent's witnesses that you want to negate by slipping into your direct examination. Review all of the relevant documents so that you have a firm grasp on what they mean and how they can help or hurt you.

Though you don't know precisely what your opponent's witnesses will say, you should have a pretty good idea. Focus before the trial starts on the facts you want to bring out in cross-examination. In particular, identify the documents you can use against your adversary.

As you prepare your script, be mindful of the double-edged sword. Documents often contain both good and bad information. Some facts can help or hurt depending on how they are used. As you isolate the evidence that supports you, do not ignore the ways it can be used against you.

You probably know the facts better than your lawyer. Take an active role in assembling the evidence. Tell him what you think is important and why. Show him critical documents. Discuss the facts you want to emphasize. Remind him of the bad facts so that you can minimize their impact. Work as partners in writing the script.

Select the Cast

You must decide who will tell your story and the order in which they will tell it. There may be many witnesses to an automobile accident, many workers who built a defective product or many employees who saw improper sexual advances by a boss. Since you generally want to keep your act in the play short and sweet, you won't call every possible witness. You want only the most credible.

> "From a plot hatched in hell, don't expect angels for witnesses."
>
> —Robert Perry

You probably know the strengths and weaknesses of your potential witnesses better than your lawyer. Work with him to select the witnesses who will best present your case. Though every case and witness is different, the following principles may apply:

Witnesses Should Be Knowledgeable

The most credible witness is not always the most senior or the best salesperson. She is usually the one with the most knowledge. She should be a person at the center of the controversy, not a peripheral player. You don't want a witness to admit repeatedly on cross-examination that someone else knows more than she does. The jury will not rely on her testimony and may wonder why you even called her.

Your witness must also be competent to introduce your evidence. If you rely on key letters, memoranda, or contracts, the witnesses must be able to authenticate them. If you plan to show the jury photographs of an automobile accident, the witness must be able to testify that the photographs accurately depict the crash scene.

If your witness can't get your evidence admitted, she has no value.

The Jury Should Identify with Your Witnesses

Your chief executive officer may not be persuasive to an hourly assembly line worker from a company implementing substantial layoffs or a mother of eight subsisting on welfare. The jury may identify more closely with a low-level employee "laboring in the vineyard." However, don't educate a witness who doesn't know the facts firsthand in the hope that he will "fit in" with the jury. Even an average cross-examination will demonstrate that this witness is "all show" and diminish the credibility of your case.

You should also consider the personality of your witnesses. For example, you don't want to begin your case with someone who is rude to everyone he meets. The jury won't like him or you. Similarly, you don't want to call a naturally nervous person who may not appear credible even when telling the truth. To the extent that you can, call witnesses who are honest, forthright, calm, warm, and convincing.

Witnesses Should Speak Clearly and Concisely

Since most of your case will be communicated through oral testimony, at the risk of stating the obvious, your witnesses must speak clearly. They should also be able to make a focused, direct presentation of the evidence that supports your theme.

Witnesses Should Answer the Question

Witnesses who don't answer your questions or, more important, don't answer questions on cross-examination, can be a disaster. Witnesses who ramble on about whatever they want are confusing at best. At worst, they appear evasive. They lack the credibility necessary to convince the jury that your act in the play is true.

Senior executive officers are often terrible witnesses. They are used to asking questions and giving orders, not answering questions. Some salesmen are spectacular on direct examination as they pitch your story, but are destroyed on cross because they don't answer the precise questions being asked and appear nonresponsive.

The Cast for Your Play

A good witness is:

- ☐ Credible
- ☐ Confident
- ☐ Articulate
- ☐ A good listener
- ☐ Responsive
- ☐ Knowledgeable
- ☐ Patient
- ☐ Calm
- ☐ Able to stick to his guns
- ☐ Sincere
- ☐ Truthful

Witnesses Should Listen

You can't answer the question if you don't hear and understand it. Many witnesses lack the concentration necessary to focus consistently on the many questions asked in direct and cross-examination. Since the questions determine the direction and flow of your production, a witness who doesn't understand your questions cannot effectively tell your story.

Adverse Witnesses

You may prove your case through your opponent's witnesses. This can be dangerous in that their goal is to reinforce your adversary's theme, not yours. Since they may be difficult to control, and may not give you the answers you anticipate, you cannot rely on them as much as your own witnesses.

Non-party Witnesses

You can also use witnesses who are not related to either side. As with a deposition, anyone can be subpoenaed to testify, provided that they live close enough to the court. Before you subpoena someone to testify on your behalf, interview them first. For example, Samantha Baker filed a sexual harassment claim against her former boss. One of Samantha's former co-workers said that the boss repeatedly made lewd comments about her in the men's room. When Samantha subpoenaed the co-worker to testify three years later, he denied ever hearing any lewd remarks. When confronted with his prior statement to Samantha, he said that he was a "born again" Christian, that his prior statement was a lie, and that he was now telling the truth. Needless to say, Samantha should have discovered this before, not after, she issued the subpoena.

Deposition Testimony

If witnesses live too far from the court to be subpoenaed and won't voluntarily appear, take their deposition for use at trial. You can read the deposition transcript in court as if it were live testimony. Even more effective is to show a videotape of the witness at the deposition.

Make Your Lineup

The order in which you call your witnesses is extremely important. They must tell your story in a logical sequence. For this reason, most acts begin with a key witness who was in the thick of things from beginning to end. He provides a framework for all subsequent evidence.

Primacy and recency apply to the order of witnesses. This theory assumes that jurors remember best the evidence they hear first and last, but pay less attention to everything in between. For this reason, most directors call the most important witnesses at the beginning and end of their act, and the supporting cast fills the middle.

Whatever order you select, make sure that your witnesses stand ready. Few judges will recess a trial while you bring your witnesses to court. Though this may not be a problem with witnesses under your control, if you are relying on non-party witnesses, subpoena them to make sure they're in court when you need them.

Rehearsal

You and all of your witnesses should practice your testimony. Unexpected questions and answers can lead to surprises that undercut your theme. Have your lawyer ask questions so that you can rehearse your answers. Anticipate your opponent's cross-examination so that you're not flustered by her questions. If you've been deposed, read and reread your deposition transcript so that you know precisely what you've said before to avoid inconsistent testimony at trial. Videotape your rehearsal. Assess how you will look to the jury. Identify ways to improve your delivery. Though you can't teach a pig to sing—make a bad witness good—a little rehearsal can go a long way.

Props

Demonstrative evidence visually communicates your point. For example, Clayton Robinson claimed that he was beaten by Billy Hurst for 13 minutes in the stands at Yankee Stadium. According to the complaint, Billy drank eight 24-ounce beers without a trip to the men's room and then pounded Clayton for 13 minutes. At trial, Billy admitted a squabble but contended that Clayton's version of reality was grossly exaggerated.

Rather than simply argue that no one could drink 192 ounces of beer without going to the bathroom, and that no one could fight in the stands at Yankee Stadium for 13 nonstop minutes, Billy showed the jury. First, he put eight 24-ounce cups on a table in front of the jury box and proceeded to fill each cup slowly and dramatically with water. By the time he was done, a number of jurors were sitting with their legs crossed and squeezed together. When the last drop was poured, the jury asked for a short recess. Each juror learned in a very personal way that no one could drink 192 ounces of liquid without going to the bathroom.

Billy next put Clayton on the witness stand. He pulled out a stopwatch and asked Clayton to describe second by second what happened over the entire 13 minutes. Clayton first said that Billy hit him, pushed him down, and hit him again. Clayton again said that Billy hit him, pushed him down, and hit him again. Clayton repeated himself four or five more times, all of which consumed a total of three minutes. After three or four minutes of silence, the judge told Billy that he had made his point, and Billy sat down. These two demonstrations proved more than all hours of the verbal testimony that Clayton's wild exaggeration was not reliable.

As you prepare your act in the play, consider simulations, props, or other demonstrations that you can use to communicate your theme. In trials, a good picture truly is worth a thousand words. If your leg was shattered in an automobile accident, use a skeleton to demonstrate where and how your bones were broken. If, like Margaret Dalton, you contend that the defendant is polluting your property, show the jury a jar of the encroaching muck so that they fully appreciate your disgust. If you argue that you lost millions of dollars in profits because of the unfair business practices of a competitor, present a chart with a line running down which shows that the defendant is driving your business into the ground. If your house burned down because of faulty wiring, show the jury pictures of your destroyed home, don't just tell them that it burned. O. J. Simpson may have won his criminal trial because the glove was too small—"If it doesn't fit you must acquit." Demonstrative evidence allows you to touch the emotions of the jury more than words ever can.

Documents

Though documents are evidence, in many ways they should be treated like props. I'm often surprised at the failure of lawyers to communicate the content of important documents to juries. Many lawyers hand the "smoking gun" document to a witness on the stand, ask the witness to read portions to the jury and then go on with the rest of case. The jury never studies the document while the case is proceeding. The document is not emphasized. Unless the jurors are extremely attentive, the document blends in with all of the other evidence. The jury may miss the import of the document all together.

You may want to blow up important documents, glue them to a foam board and put them on an easel directly in front of the jury box so that the jury can read them. You can also copy the documents onto transparencies and show them on an overhead projector. You can scan them into a personal computer and project them onto a screen, enlarging critical portions. Or, you a can give each juror a copy. You can also underline or highlight important portions of the document. Whatever you select, make sure that the jury not only hears about the document, but also reads and studies it.

Costume Design

Clothes communicate an image. Since the jury sees you long before it hears you, your first impression can affect the jury's perception of you throughout the trial. You need to look your part. If you are a successful businessman, dress like a modest but successful businessman. If you've been out of a job for two years and are down on your luck, dress with simple dignity. Don't use clothes to give the impression you're someone you're not.

A high-flying stockbroker was charged with churning the investment accounts of his customers. He came to court every day in brown slacks and a blue cotton sweater. He attempted to portray the image of the middle-class neighbor next door, not the Wall Street wheeler-dealer. His opponent spent the first 10 minutes of cross-examination inquiring about his high-priced, custom-made suits from Hong Kong, French designer ties, and Italian loafers. By the time cross-examination was over, the jury felt that he was the fraud his customers claimed him to be.

Though you should dress your part, you also want to identify with the jury. If you normally wear fancy clothes, dress down. Had the stockbroker worn a simple suit and tie, he could have rebutted any claim that he was attempting to manufacture an image, yet at the same time would have looked like a "regular guy."

An economic expert we retained from a Big Six accounting firm walked into court wearing a double-breasted suit, a striped shirt with collar pin and cuff links, and tasseled loafers. He looked very sharp and very high priced. We sent him home to put on black tie shoes, a single-breasted suit, and a shirt with buttons.

Set Design

Your options for set design are limited. The judge sits behind the bench, the witness on the witness stand, the jury in the jury box,

Trial Prep Checklist

Review and comply with any pretrial order.

- ☐ Draft your theme.
- ☐ Review all depositions.
- ☐ Read your documents.
- ☐ Read your adversary's documents.
- ☐ Select facts for your script.
- ☐ Identify your witnesses.
- ☐ Select the order of witnesses.
- ☐ Select deposition excerpts.
- ☐ Select your exhibits.
- ☐ Make lots of copies of exhibits.
- ☐ Prepare your props.
- ☐ Prepare witness examinations.
- ☐ Subpoena witnesses.
- ☐ Practice your testimony.
- ☐ Prepare legal memoranda or jury instructions.

and you and your lawyer behind a table. You can modify the set in small ways to help the jury identify with you, however.

You and your lawyer should increase your opportunities to stand up and walk around in front of the jury. For example, come down from the witness stand to point to critical portions of documents, photographs, or maps that are blown up and sitting on an easel in front of the jury box. Write on a large pad or blackboard before the jury. Stand before the jury in full view. You seem more human. You increase your rapport with the jury. By moving around, you also break up the monotony of a witness droning on from the witness stand. You cause the jury to pay more attention to your case.

Presenting the Law

No trial would be complete without a thorough presentation of the law. In a bench trial, judges often request a pretrial memorandum that outlines the issues in the case and the law that applies. Others may require proposed findings of fact and conclusions of law that outline the decision you want the judge to reach at the end of the trial. As with any other legal memorandum or brief, your arguments should be clear, concise and to the point.

In a jury trial, you submit to the judge proposed jury instructions that set out the law the jury is supposed to consider and apply in reaching its decision. Many instructions are accepted, generic charges. This is particularly true with legal issues that arise in almost every case, including the burden of proof and the weight of evidence. There are also pattern jury instructions for common types of claims such as automobile-accident and slip-and-fall claims.

There are also unique legal issues in most cases. Your lawyer should draft proposed instructions to present these principles to the jury. The law is contained in decisions written by judges in prior cases. Since different judges describe the law in different ways, the key to drafting jury instructions is to find decisions in terms that are more favorable to you than your opponent. Phrases from these decisions will be the core of your instructions. After each side presents its proposed jury instructions to the court, the judge drafts his own instructions often based on a composite of the submissions of the parties.

Picking Your Audience Part 2: Jury Selection

After four years, the time has come for Amanda Peterson to try her $15 million case against Sycamore Machine over the death of her husband, Mark, in an assembly line accident. Sycamore has refused to pay enough to cover a lifetime of expenses for Amanda and her four children because it claims it did nothing wrong. Amanda is betting that a jury will give her enough to provide for the rest of her life. She is filled with hope as she walks into the courtroom for trial, only to confront 45 people she has never seen before. From this subdued, anonymous group will come the jury that may dictate the rest of her life.

Voir dire (to speak the truth) is the name for jury selection. It is also the first time the jury sees you. Since first impressions are important, you should get off on the right foot.

Voir dire varies widely. In some courts, your lawyer cannot talk directly with prospective jurors. In these jurisdictions, you receive a form which provides general information about each juror, including the juror's age, race, ethnic origin, education, sex, and occupation. This information and perhaps answers to a few questions from the judge are all of the facts you have to evaluate prospective jurors. Your decision to exclude jurors is based largely upon your own stereotypes about the biases of different races, ethnic groups, sexes, age groups, or occupations. You must rely upon your assumptions about how a white school teacher or a Hispanic policeman would react to your case.

For example, Dick Mercer was sued for stealing money from his corporation and falsifying books and records to cover up the theft. One of the potential jurors was the manager of the homeowner claims fraud unit of a major insurance company. Dick knew solely from her occupation that she would want to sniff out a fraud. He excluded her as soon as he had the chance. Similarly, if you are being sued by a bank, you probably don't want a banker on the jury. Amanda Peterson may who want on her jury young fathers who would project on Amanda images of their wives and sympathize with her effort to keep her family together.

In other jurisdictions, *voir dire* is virtually unlimited. Your lawyer can talk with prospective jurors about almost anything he wants. Because it is the only time in the case that your lawyer and the jurors can converse with each other, take advantage of it.

A key to *voir dire* is to put jurors at ease. Your lawyer should ask broad, non-threatening, general questions to get them talking. She should discuss their lives with them. Since the jurors identify your lawyer with you, through this dialogue, you will become comfortable with each other. You want the jury to know you—to feel like you are "their kind of person." If you are a plaintiff, you hope the jury will empathize with you. Your goal is to cause them to want to give you substantial amounts of money. If you are a defendant, you want the jury to understand you, what you did and why. You hope they will conclude that they would have done exactly the same thing.

Since *voir dire* is also the beginning of your attempt to persuade the jury that you should win, your lawyer should clearly and concisely present your theme. Your lawyer's discussion with jurors should amplify and reinforce this theme. Observe the way jurors respond to it. You want to keep jurors who like the theme and excuse those who don't buy it.

In the context of these two overriding issues of dialogue and theme, keep in mind the following:

Get to Know the Jurors

Find out in *voir dire* who the jurors are. What do they like? What do they dislike? How have they experienced life? What are the key events? One of my partners asks potential jurors about the last book they read. One man once replied that it was the autobiography of Adolf Hitler. He said that Hitler made a lot of good points. He was excluded ASAP.

Get Jurors to Identify with You

Your lawyer should explore with jurors their experiences that are similar to yours. Discussion of these common events causes jurors to identify with you. You can also incorporate analogies to a juror's personal experiences into your script to touch more precisely that juror's emotions.

These discussions can also break down barriers to identification. For example, if the defendant is a big corporation in a "David versus Goliath" case, and one of the potential jurors works for a huge corporation, a dialogue about the juror's fellow workers, and the fact that a large corporation is nothing more than a collection of people working together to do their jobs the best way they can, helps humanize the corporation and minimize the "big guy–little guy" aspect of a case.

Your lawyer shouldn't "show off" in front of the jury. Your lawyer shouldn't use big words or quote Shakespeare. You want to be identified with the neighbor next door. You should impress the jury with how average you are, not how great you are.

Use the Dialogue to Present Your Theme

Your lawyer should use *voir dire* to communicate your theme. For example, Henry Burk slashed his hand with a hedge cutter. He sued the manufacturer, claiming that the hedge cutter was defective. In *voir dire*, Henry's lawyer discussed with each juror the products they bought over their lives that didn't work and why. This dialogue conditioned the jurors to think about defective products and the rights and frustrations of those who buy them. The theme of defective products was pervasive. The discussion increased juror receptivity to Henry's position and the likelihood that he would prevail.

Be Respectful

Nobody likes to be talked down to. When dealing with a jury—a group of people whom you want to like you—your lawyer should be respectful. He should ask questions in a way that enhances a juror's dignity. If a juror is a garbage man, your lawyer should ask him to describe his employment history, not say, "Have you really been a garbage man for 20 years?" Your lawyer may want to ask women on the jury whether they prefer Miss, Ms., or Mrs. He should say "please" and "thank you." He should show that you and he care about and respect the jury's opinions and values.

This does not mean that your lawyer should pander to the jury. He doesn't want to thank the Adolf Hitler fan for "sharing" his views. The other members of the jury pool will see right through him. Though he should be polite, he must retain his self-respect.

Establish and Maintain Credibility

Since credibility is the key to persuasion, your lawyer must at the beginning of *voir dire* begin to build credibility. The jury may be skeptical of both of you. Your lawyer must convince the jurors to trust you. She shouldn't talk too much. She shouldn't overstate or oversell your case. If she promises too much, and the evidence does not back you up, then everything you and she say throughout the rest of the trial will be questioned.

Be Yourself

Most jurors know a snake-oil salesman when they see one. A lawyer should stay within himself. If he's not funny, he shouldn't tell jokes. If he's naturally light-hearted and gregarious, he shouldn't create an atmosphere of false seriousness.

Be Direct

Though your lawyer wants to be respectful, she also needs to get to the point. If she represents Amanda Peterson, she should ask whether the jurors believe that the defendants are responsible for their actions and, if so, whether the jurors believe that the defendants should pay. Your lawyer might also ask whether they object to a million-dollar verdict awarded to a man who buys a scratched BMW or a woman who burns herself with hot coffee from McDonald's. She should determine whether they have any biases against awarding substantial damages.

Sycamore Machine's lawyer might admit that Amanda Peterson's situation is tragic, but ask whether a defendant who did nothing wrong should be held responsible. He may inquire about the impact on business if those who are innocent have to solve all problems or "right all wrongs." He could ask the jurors how they would feel if they worked for Sycamore Machine.

Discuss the Law

Your case may ultimately be decided on the jury's application of the law to the facts. Your lawyer should describe the law in *voir dire*. He should ask jurors if they will apply the law the way you want them to if you prove your case.

Disclose Your Weaknesses

Your lawyer should disclose any significant problems up front. You don't want the jury to be shocked midway through the trial after you have carefully built a persuasive and credible case. Put the dirty laundry on the table at the beginning to avoid unwelcome surprises.

Watch and Listen

Listen to what the jurors say. Don't make the mistake of focusing on the next question, your opponent, or your opponent's lawyer. Juror answers are the keys to their personalities. They may also open the door to further dialogue which your lawyer can use to elicit useful information or develop your theme.

Observe how the jurors act. Listen to the tones of their voices as they respond to questions. Watch the body language. Does a juror smile or frown? Are her arms tightly crossed in a defensive position or hanging peacefully at her side? How does she interrelate with her fellow jurors? Pay attention to the "vibes" you get. Trust your intuition. Body language is often much more telling than anything a juror says.

Create the Right Atmosphere

Jury selection is a time to begin creating an atmosphere that is conducive to your case. If you are a plaintiff, you want the jury to feel that a great wrong has been committed. Don't kid around with your opponent. Don't let the jury think that you are friends and that the dispute is not serious. On the other hand, if you are the defendant, be friendly to everyone you see. Try to strike up a conversation with your opponent. The jury should sense that the case is no big deal.

Know When to Stop

If you find a juror you like, your lawyer should stop talking to him. The more your lawyer reinforces the belief that the juror is good for you, the more she convinces your opponent that the juror is bad for him. If you find someone you like, move on to the next juror as soon as possible.

Follow a Plan

Create a plan for *voir dire*. List in advance the points you want your lawyer to cover. *Voir dire* should follow a logical sequence, beginning with a discussion of juror biographies and closing with questions designed to emphasize the strengths of your case. Your lawyer should incorporate your theme throughout. If he doesn't use a plan, he may meander around a few hours, having learned little about the jurors and persuading no one of anything.

Selecting the Jury

Jury selection begins when the clerk of court identifies an initial group from the jury pool for your jury. Throughout the *voir dire* process, you consider whether you want to replace anyone in this group with others from the jury pool.

You have a limited number of peremptory challenges that allow you to knock a juror off the panel for any reason. You need no justification—a hostile look in your direction may be all it takes. However, since you have few peremptory challenges, you should use them carefully.

You have an unlimited number of challenges "for cause." If a juror works for your adversary, or already knows about the case and says he can't be fair and honest, you may be able to exclude him for cause. Since you want to save your peremptory challenges as long as you can, first attempt to remove a juror "for cause."

Keep track of the number of challenges you and your opponent use. You don't want to be caught without a peremptory challenge when the juror from hell is put on the panel. Similarly, you don't through inattention want to give your adversary an extra peremptory challenge.

As you exercise your challenges, do not ignore the potential jurors remaining. You don't want to use a peremptory challenge on a so-so juror who may be replaced by your worst nightmare.

Who Do You Want on the Jury?

Though a Jungian jury consultant armed with a computer may tell you otherwise, picking a jury is more art than science. There are some universal assumptions based on stereotypes. For example, men supposedly are more responsive to a female personal-injury plaintiff and vice versa. Ethnic groups give more to plaintiffs. Bankers and accountants are good for defendants, whereas salesmen and teachers are good for plaintiffs. Though you can stereotype each of your prospective jurors, you never really know in advance how someone will react to your case.

Ultimately you want jurors who will identify with you and your case. They should understand where you're coming from and why you are where you are. You want jurors who will care about you. Sycamore Machine wants jurors who understand business. Amanda Peterson wants jurors who understand families.

Your lawyer has no monopoly on picking the right jury. You can spot a warm smile or a cold frown as well as your lawyer. Use your instincts. Trust your intuition. Be active, don't just rely on your lawyer.

Did You Make the Right Choice?

Though oftentimes you have no idea how well you're doing, pay close attention to the judge or jury to see if you are communicating your theme. Does the jury scowl when your witnesses are on the stand? Do they sleep through the afternoon? Is the judge attentive to your case, or is she filling out Christmas cards? If the judge sarcastically asks your lawyer if he's ready to "resume his devastating cross-examination," you know you've got a problem.

Jury Selection Checklist

- ☐ Review biographical information on jurors.
- ☐ Relate biographical information to you and your case.
- ☐ Relate biographical information to your opponent and his case.
- ☐ Watch and listen.
- ☐ Are the jurors talking?
- ☐ How do jurors respond to your lawyer?
- ☐ How do they respond to you?
- ☐ How do they respond to your theme?
- ☐ Do you have anything in common?
- ☐ How do they respond to your opponent?
- ☐ How do they respond to your opponent's lawyer?
- ☐ How do they respond to your opponent's theme?
- ☐ Are there any positive biases?
- ☐ Are there any negative biases?
- ☐ How do jurors relate to each other?
- ☐ Trust your intuition.

One of my colleagues in his first jury trial was examining a particularly difficult witness. The witness froze on the stand. He was incapable of answering even the most simple questions. After twenty-five minutes, the lawyer heard this deep, quiet voice from the jury box grumble "Why don't you just sit down?" He did. It was time to try something different.

TRIAL: THE CURTAIN IS RAISED

Margaret Dalton waited four long years to try her case against Tom Dixon. Though a preliminary injunction required Tom to divert his septic system sludge away from her yard, he implemented only stop-gap measures that failed repeatedly. Margaret had to go back to court three times to try to make Tom stem the sewage tide. She also spent thousands of dollars cleaning up the mess. She's fed up. She wants to sell her house and move, but no one will buy it. Her only hope is to resolve the dispute once and for all in the trial.

There are four key components to the Dalton-Dixon trial play. The lawyers first make opening statements to the jury. Margaret then presents her "case in chief"—the direct examination of her witnesses, who are then cross-examined by Tom's lawyer. After Margaret "rests" her case, Tom's lawyer examines witnesses in his case in chief. These witnesses are then cross-examined by Margaret's lawyer. At the conclusion of the evidence, lawyers for each side make closing arguments to the jury.

Though opening and closing statements can be important, evidence is the key to victory. Most juries know that a lawyer's argument is little more than a sales pitch. Consequently, your case will probably be decided based on the direct and cross-examinations of the witnesses.

> "A [lawyer's] performance in the courtroom is responsible for about 25 percent of the outcome; the remaining 75 percent depends on the facts."
>
> —Melvin Belli

The versions of the truth presented by each side usually conflict, often dramatically. Truthful witnesses can perceive and recall the same events in diametrically opposed ways. If the facts weren't in dispute, you probably wouldn't be having a trial in the first place.

You may feel like you are on an emotional roller coaster as the conflicting stories unfold. If both plays are properly produced and directed, you should feel like you are scoring a lot of points with the jury when you present your evidence and cross-examine your opponent's witnesses. When your adversary is on stage, the reverse may be true. You may be afraid that you are losing badly. You may be outraged by what your opponent says about you. Keep the big picture in mind. No case is black or white; if it were, you wouldn't be in court. The fact that your opponent makes a few good points does not mean that he will prevail.

A trial is much like a five-set tennis match. You will probably win and lose many games throughout the match. Your lead witness may be great and you may win his set at love; the reverse may be true when your opponent's star is on the stand. You will probably feel the momentum shift many times throughout the match. Most cases and witnesses have good and bad moments. Don't be overly concerned. The only thing that matters is that you pull it out in the fifth set.

The Opening Statement

Though your lawyer presents your theme in *voir dire*, the opening statement is his first opportunity to explain your story from beginning to end in clear, forceful, positive language. His narrative should outline all of the important evidence the jury will hear in a way that emphasizes your theme. Your story needs to make sense; it should intuitively ring true. By the time your lawyer finishes his opening, the jury should have a thorough understanding of where you will go and how you will get there.

The opening statement is in many ways the canvas of a paint-by-numbers picture. It gives context to the testimony that will follow. It is the framework on which the jury can hang the pieces of evidence presented during the trial. It provides an outline through which the jury can understand and relate evidence to your story as a whole.

In addition to providing a context for the evidence, your lawyer should use the opening statement to enhance your credibility. Your lawyer can accomplish these goals through the following:

Be a Storyteller

Your lawyer should communicate with the jury as if she is telling a story around a campfire or in a living room. She should be personable and friendly. She should rely on simple language, not use legalese. She shouldn't use big words. She should simply tell the story of what happened and why in a calm, pleasant voice.

Don't Hide

Many lawyers literally or figuratively hide from the jury. They anchor themselves behind lecterns with only the upper parts of their torsos showing and read prepared scripts or, at the very least, from detailed notes. The jury doesn't get a sense of who they are.

Your lawyer should get out from behind the lectern so that the jury can size him up from head to toe. This will cause the jury to feel like it knows your lawyer better and can trust him and you. He shouldn't read the opening. He should keep notes to a minimum and appear spontaneous in his delivery. A story "from the heart" is more authentic than a written speech. Do not worry about imperfect language, sentence structure, or syntax. Your lawyer may even forget a fact or two. A few mistakes here and there convey the image that your lawyer is human, which all jurors are.

Humanize the Case

You want the jury to know you as a person, not as a litigant. For example, Margaret Dalton does not want to be the "plaintiff"; she wants to be the friend down the street. Sycamore Machine does not want to be an inanimate corporation; it wants to be a group of people working together to provide for their families. Your lawyer should not refer to you as the "defendant" or a "party to the litigation." She should refer to you by name. If you represent a company, she should talk about your employees. She should use the pronouns "we" and "us," not "it" and "them."

Ignore Your Opponent

Your lawyer should not waste time in the opening statement rebutting your opponent's claims. There's plenty of time to attack your adversary later. You want the jury to understand fully where you are coming from. If it doesn't, it will focus on your opponent's story, regardless of the number of holes you've poked in it.

Explain the Process

Most jurors have never seen a trial. One way to enhance your credibility is for your lawyer to explain accurately the trial play. If the jury trusts his description of the process, it may be more willing to trust the other things you and he say. By making the jury more familiar and comfortable with the trial, he may also make it more familiar and comfortable with you.

Don't Oversell

As with *voir dire,* your lawyer should not oversell your case. If he does, it will come back to haunt you. Every good lawyer pays strict attention to her opponent's opening statement. If an adversary overstates the case, she can in closing argument remind the jury of the broken promises. If the jury concludes you weren't honest in your opening, you will lose credibility.

Disclose Weaknesses

If bad facts will come out, your lawyer should work them into the story in a way that minimizes the damage. You want to avoid surprising the jury. You want to prepare the jury to conclude that the bad facts are insignificant in the context of the story as a whole.

Don't Argue

The opening statement is not an argument. Your lawyer should not tell the jury what to think. He should describe your story in a way that induces the jury to conclude on its own that you should win. An argumentative opening statement may also draw an objection, which will disrupt your lawyer's presentation and diminish its impact.

Be Visual

Since most people process information visually rather than aurally, your lawyer should communicate visually in the opening. She should ask the judge in advance if she can use props or exhibits. She should use gestures to help make his points. She shouldn't just drone on.

The First Fifty Words

The first few sentences set the tone for the rest of an opening statement. Moreover, they are the words the jury will best re-member as the trial proceeds. Your lawyer should use them to present in clear, concise, forceful, memorable language the theme of your case.

The Last Fifty Words

Your lawyer should conclude with a restatement of your theme and a request for action that the jury will remember. He should end with a bang.

Tell the Jury What You Want

Your lawyer should explain to the jury precisely what you want. She shouldn't be vague. If you want a million dollars, she should ask for a million dollars. If you want the jury to conclude that you owe nothing, she should say so. By the time the opening state-ment is over, the jury should know exactly what you expect it to do.

Resist the Urge to Object

If your lawyer objects to your opponent's opening statement, the jury may think that you are trying to disrupt his flow or hide information. This may diminish your credibility for the rest of the trial. Unless your opponent is way out of line, let him go. A bet-ter strategy may be for your lawyer to remind the jury of your adversary's aggressiveness in closing argument.

Direct Examination

You win most cases on direct examination. You generally succeed based on your strengths, not your opponent's weaknesses. An effective direct examination is a flowing narrative that details your evidence in simple, direct language the jury can understand and identify with. Emphasize your positives. Tell the story in a way that induces the jurors to understand the facts the way you want them to. Though each case and witness are different, and a direct examination must be tailored to the case and witness, a few basic principles apply:

Don't Use Leading Questions

Since the jury would rather hear from the witness than the lawyer, the witness should tell the story in narrative form. He should not mechanically affirm self-serving statements from the lawyer with a series of "yes" answers. Proper direct-examination questions include "describe the accident scene" or "explain why the sewage flowed onto Margaret Dalton's yard." Because they highlight the witness, they are much more effective than: "Isn't it true that the accident occurred at 1:42 P.M.?" or "Didn't Mr. Dixon refuse to plug the hole in the septic system?" These leading questions emphasize the lawyer, who almost by definition is less trustworthy than a witness. Moreover, they are improper under the rules of evidence and may draw objections.

Rhythm and Pace

The witness should not put the jury to sleep with one long monologue. The lawyer should vary the pace by alternating questions that elicit short, crisp answers with those that seek long, descriptive answers. Changes in rhythm and pace keep the jury alert. They help the jury to focus on and remember your evidence.

Don't Waste Time

A jury is a group of people forced to endure your troubles against their will. If your trial team is disorganized, inefficient, slow, or simply wastes time, the jury may resent you, which means you will probably lose. Move the trial as quickly as possible.

Emphasize Key Facts

When you want to emphasize a key fact, your lawyer should change pace and slow down. He should ask a number of questions that relate to that fact. The more time he spends on a fact, the greater the chance the jury will remember it.

Use Silence

If you get a blockbuster answer, your lawyer should pause for a moment. She should let it hang in the air. Though perhaps a little dramatic, the pause may allow the answer to sink into the jurors' minds. She shouldn't overdo it, however. One lawyer who I've seen inhales and exhales loudly every time he gets a good answer. He looks ridiculous.

Use Simple Language

Questions must be asked and answered in language everyone understands. For example, a lawyer named Jones examined a woman seeking an uncontested divorce. The woman had to prove that she and her husband did not "cohabit" within the preceding six months. As he was running through the examination, Jones asked, "And when was the last time you cohabited?" The woman replied, "Why last night with you, lawyer Jones." Any question can be asked and answered in simple language. For example, "live together" is a reasonable substitute for "cohabit." Simplicity means clarity and credibility.

Keep Questions Short

Short questions are clear. The jury and the witness can follow them. Moreover, they don't draw objections, which can break up your flow and divert the jury from your story.

Cross-Examination

The purpose of cross-examination is to challenge your opponent's act in the play in two principal ways. First, you want the witness to agree with you as much as possible in order to narrow the dispute and emphasize those facts that your adversary admits support your case. Second, if the witness hurts you, you want to discredit his testimony. Though cross-examination may appear difficult, adherence to a few basic rules makes it easier than direct examination.

Lead the Witness

Contrary to direct examination, a cardinal rule of cross-examination is to lead the witness. Leading questions are those which suggest the answer and permit only a "yes" or "no" response. For example, "The sun was shining at the time of the accident, wasn't it?" is leading. A non-leading version of the same question is "Describe the weather at the time of the accident."

A leading question is a self-serving statement with a question at the end. For example, if you need to prove the sun was shining at the time of the accident, your lawyer could state, "The sun was shining at the time of the accident," and then add, "isn't that correct?" to make it a question. Leading questions allow an examiner to tell the story in her own language, not the language of the witness. Through these questions, your lawyer highlights those facts that help you that your opponent agrees with. If your lawyer simply states the facts that support your case, and begins each statement with "Isn't it true that," you have the basis of a decent cross-examination.

Take Small Steps

The leading questions should be small, crisp, short statements. You want clear, unambiguous questions that the witness can't waffle on. You don't want the witness to say that he can't answer the question "yes" or "no," or to claim that he doesn't understand the question. Your lawyer should ask questions that you know the witness must respond "yes" to very quickly.

Develop a Rhythm

By asking short, simple questions eliciting "yes" answers, your lawyer develops a fast-paced rhythm of statement-answer, statement-answer. The witness gets in the habit of saying "yes." Lawyer and witness get in a flow. Lots of "yes" answers may leave the jury with the impression that the witness agrees with you on all major points.

Control the Witness

If your lawyer asks a leading question, she is entitled to a "yes" or "no" answer. But many adverse witnesses don't want to give this response. They want to make long, self-serving speeches. They want to tell their story their way. They want to answer their questions, not yours. There are a number of ways to control this type of witness. The judge can strike the answer. Your lawyer can keep asking the same question over and over until it is answered, highlighting the witness's evasiveness. She can also ask the witness why he refuses to respond to the question, or whether his lawyer told him not to answer. All of these techniques should embarrass the witness and bring him under control.

Don't Argue

The jury knows that the lawyer is dominant in the examiner-witness relationship. When lawyer and witness argue, the lawyer, not the witness, usually looks bad in the eyes of the jury.

Be Confident

Attitude is important. If your lawyer is confident and assertive, the witness will feel like he is in control and be less willing to fight. If your lawyer is tentative, the witness may sense weakness and try to take over.

Know the Answer to the Question

A lawyer shouldn't ask a question if he doesn't know the answer. He may be surprised. Jack Ryan was defending an automobile accident case. Though the plaintiff had no apparent physical injury, he claimed that his back hurt and he couldn't sleep at night. Near the close of his cross-examination, Jack loudly barked, "You don't know what suffering is, do you?" The man calmly stood, rolled up his sleeve and showed the jury a number tatooed on his arm in a concentration camp. The case settled shortly thereafter.

Focus on the Big Points

Use cross-examination to highlight the major points that help your case. Your lawyer should not waste time on insignificant facts. He shouldn't question everything the witness said on direct. He shouldn't allow the witness to repeat his direct examination or emphasize his good facts. He also shouldn't cross-examine a witness too long because a witness's ability to respond to piercing questions will increase.

Don't Open the Door

After your lawyer finishes a cross-examination, your opponent's lawyer can inquire in redirect examination about subjects raised by the cross. If your adversary does not adequately cover evidence on direct examination, your lawyer should not mention it on cross so that your opponent cannot clarify the evidence on redirect.

Don't Ask the Extra Question

If you get a good answer, leave it alone. Abraham Lincoln reputedly defended a man accused of biting off the ear of another. During Lincoln's cross-examination, the prosecution's witness admitted that it was dark and that he didn't actually see the defendant bite off the ear. Lincoln then mistakenly asked the extra question: "Then you don't actually know that he bit off the ear, do you?" The answer was, "Yes, I saw him spit it out."

Use Questions to Make Arguments

Your lawyer should at times ask conclusory questions that highlight your theme, even though you know the answer will be "no." He asks these questions to remind the jury of that theme and how the witness's testimony fits into it.

Give a Witness Plenty of Rope

There is in every trial a difficult, evasive, or dishonest witness. Let him hang himself. For example, Dick Mercer was asked repeatedly about his company's sales figures for 1994. He said he couldn't remember specifically. He said he couldn't remember generally. He said he wasn't sure. Though the examiner appeared to be getting nowhere, he persevered. When Dick was asked for a "ballpark figure," he said, "6 to 3 in the bottom of the 8th." Dick never gave the sales figures. The jury thought he was dishonest, which was far more damaging than the sales figures themselves.

Impeachment

Impeachment is the process of undercutting the credibility of a witness. If done well, it can be devastating. The litany of impeachment is to elicit from the witness clear, certain testimony. Your lawyer may want to ask the witness to confirm that he is absolutely certain that his answer is correct. Your lawyer then confronts the witness with a prior inconsistent statement in either a deposition transcript or document. A lawyer should be precise in impeachment so the jury understands that the witness has changed his story. Your lawyer should make sure that the inconsistent statement directly contradicts the trial testimony.

You should not waste time with impeachment on insignificant inconsistencies. The jury knows that nobody remembers everything. Unless the contradiction is significant and the fact is important to the case, impeachment may not be worth the trouble.

> "Liars are like snakes. Sooner or later they shed their skin. The cross-examiner's job is to make a few small incisions that will help them do this right in front of the jury. Cross-examination is a process in which you loosen the witness's skin."
>
> —Mike Ficaro

Don't Be Mean

Some lawyers are simply too aggressive on cross-examination. They tear into a witness on every little inconsistency in the hope of beating her into the ground. Avon Hydraulic's lawyer attacked the plaintiff in an age discrimination case repeatedly and mercilessly over every single insignificant, inconsistent statement. If the witness testified that a meeting occurred on Wednesday, but in fact it was on Tuesday, the lawyer grilled the witness as if it were the world's biggest lie. The assault continued for an entire day. By the end of the cross-examination, the jury hated Avon Hydraulic and its lawyer. Avon Hydraulic's lawyer's hostility turned an otherwise so-so plaintiff's case into a million-dollar claim.

Plant Seeds

Your lawyer may ask questions on cross that do not relate to the direct examination, to plant seeds for the future. These questions fill in portions of your paint-by-numbers picture that may not appear to fit in when asked, but which integrate with the whole when the picture is finished. These questions cause the jury to think. They engage them in your case. With hope, these questions will increase the likelihood that the jurors will figure out what's going on without you having to tell them.

How to Be a Good Witness

Many of the rules that apply to being a good witness at a deposition apply at trial. Listen carefully to the question, think about your answer, and respond as clearly, simply, and directly as possible. Always tell the truth. Answer only the question asked, not the question you wish had been asked. Be professional, polite, and respectful. Don't use slang. Don't make snide remarks. Don't tell jokes. Just tell it like it is.

A major difference between a trial and a deposition is that your audience is now the jury or judge, not your opponent. Look at them periodically. Tell your story directly to them. Remember that they are the only audience you care about.

Direct Examination

You are the star on direct examination. The more you say, and the less your lawyer says, the more credible your case. The best direct examination is when the lawyer fades away. Direct examination is your chance to sell your story; go for it.

Cross-Examination

As in a deposition, a witness on cross-examination should adopt the rope-a-dope philosophy. Listen carefully to the question asked, think about it, and answer only that question. If the question calls for a "yes" or "no" answer, give a "yes" or "no" answer. If you can't answer "yes" or "no," simply say you can't answer "yes" or "no." Don't give speeches. Don't make self-serving statements that aren't responsive. Admit bad facts if directly asked. Don't fight with the lawyer. Maintain your dignity and credibility. Stay calm, and keep cool.

Witness Checklist

- ☐ Know your deposition cold.
- ☐ Know key documents cold.
- ☐ Rehearse your testimony.
- ☐ Listen to the entire question.
- ☐ Think before you answer.
- ☐ Answer only the specific question asked.
- ☐ Set your own pace.
- ☐ Be precise.
- ☐ Don't use slang.
- ☐ Don't speculate.
- ☐ Be succinct.
- ☐ Admit what you don't know.
- ☐ Admit bad facts.
- ☐ Correct your mistakes.
- ☐ Read documents carefully.
- ☐ Be professional.
- ☐ Be polite.
- ☐ Keep cool.
- ☐ Don't fight.
- ☐ Don't rush.
- ☐ Look at the jury.
- ☐ Eat.
- ☐ Sleep.
- ☐ Tell the truth.

You should set the pace. Don't let the lawyer push you into a rhythm of rapid-fire questions and answers. Pause before you respond. Give yourself time to think. Give your lawyer time to object. If presented with a document, read it carefully before answering. You don't want to make a mistake because you are rushing to get off the witness stand.

Forgotten Facts

Even though you've practiced your direct examination and prepared for cross, you will probably not remember everything. If you forget information you once knew, the examining lawyer can refresh your recollection by showing you something to spark your memory. For example, if you forgot that you received a letter, the lawyer can show you a copy and ask if it refreshes your recollection that you once received it. If it does, say so. If it doesn't, stick to your guns, even though the letter may have your name on it.

Correcting Mistakes

If you give testimony that you subsequently realize is inaccurate, tell your lawyer. Correct your testimony as soon as you can. Don't leave false testimony on the record.

Eat and Sleep

Testifying is stressful and exhausting. You will burn up significant amounts of energy. Lou Fisher turned white and nearly passed out on the stand because he skipped breakfast. Carl Smith testified after flying all night from the west coast. By 4 P.M., he was incoherent.

Foundations

You will hear much about foundations throughout the trial. A foundation is a fact or group of facts that must be proved before you can introduce evidence. For example, to introduce a conversation, a witness should state who spoke to whom, when, and where. To introduce an interoffice memorandum, a witness should testify to the date of the document, the author of the document, and whether it was prepared and kept in the ordinary course of business. Though perhaps boring, these foundational litanies must be completed before presenting evidence to the jury. If your lawyer doesn't lay a proper foundation, evidence is not admissible over your opponent's objection.

Rebuttal

Since you have no control over your opponent's case, there will always be unexpected evidence. You have the right to respond with your own evidence.

Since the defendant goes second, she can respond to surprises from the plaintiff during his case in chief. The plaintiff, on the other hand, must present additional evidence in his rebuttal case after the defendant has completed her act of the play. The plaintiff is not allowed to retry his case. He should only respond to evidence from the defendant.

Objections

You have the right to object to improper questions and inadmissible evidence. If an objection is sustained, the witness may not answer the question and the jury cannot consider the evidence.

Many clients believe that their lawyers do not object enough. Some clients want to object to any negative evidence, even if it is admissible. Lawyers, on the other hand, often allow their opponent to introduce inadmissible facts.

Though you have a right to object, you may not want to. The jury wants to know all of the facts. If you object too much, the jury may think you're trying to hide something, particularly if the judge overrules your objection. Moreover, an objection communicates to the jury that the evidence is important to your adversary. If you object and lose, you may emphasize a bad fact.

Your attorney may want to object to disrupt your opponent's rhythm. If he's on a roll, a couple of well-timed objections can break his momentum. Of course, don't make frivolous objections simply for the sake of disrupting your adversary. You may get a forceful "overruled" and a stern look from the judge, which may diminish your credibility in front of the jury.

When You're Not on the Stand

You should assume that the jury sees and hears everything that happens during the trial. If you groan or frown when your opponent questions your ethics, the jury will see it. If you whisper nervously in your lawyer's ear, or frantically scribble notes and hand them to your lawyer, the jury may conclude that you don't like what you hear. Be aware that everything you do or say in the courtroom sends a message. Be calm and professional, and keep a straight face.

We represented a large corporate defendant in a lawsuit in which the plaintiff claimed that we committed unfair and deceptive trade practices. Throughout the trial, the lawyers and the judge told war stories and jokes in front of the jury. The employees of the two companies talked together when the jurors came in and out of the courtroom. From the jury's perspective, the plaintiff, defendant, and judge were friends. The jury did not sense any hostility. This friendly atmosphere contributed to our win.

Closing Argument

Closing argument is the grand finale. Use it to pull all of the evidence together under the umbrella of your theme to explain why you should win.

Some lawyers organize a closing argument in a very straightforward way. This approach can be described as "tell them where you're going, go there, and tell them where you went." While this methodology generally leads to an excellent summary of the evidence, it may lack the flexibility for a great closing.

In addition to recounting much of the evidence, others rely more heavily on stories, analogies, and rhetorical questions that relate to and emphasize the theme. These techniques cause the jury to think. More important, they enable the jury to relate your case and theme to their personal experiences. They increase your chances of touching the jury's emotions, thereby enhancing your chances of victory.

Whichever strategy you adopt, as with the opening statement, your lawyer should keep the closing simple, short, direct, and to the point. KISS applies. He should not try to cover too much. He should emphasize the highlights. He should be visual. He should use exhibits as much as possible to break up the monotony of his speech. He should not use notes. He should tell your story as if in a conversation. He should not hide behind a lectern. He should not oversell your case. He should admit your obvious weaknesses while explaining why you should win. He should maintain credibility.

Unlike the opening, your lawyer should in closing respond to your opponent. He should highlight evidence that undercuts your adversary's case. He should identify flaws in the other side's analysis. He should explain why your opponent's theme doesn't make sense.

The Wait

After the closing arguments, the judge reads the instructions to the jury and you must wait for the jury to decide. Sometimes you must wait for days. You cannot hurry the process. It may be time to read that novel that you haven't had a chance to start.

Your wait may be much longer if the judge will decide your case. Judges generally request post-trial memoranda in which the parties summarize and argue the facts and the law. Months can pass before the briefing is completed and the judge renders a decision.

THE FAT LADY HASN'T SUNG **18**

There is a loud knock on the jury room door. The jurors have reached a verdict. Amanda Peterson and Eric Abelson, the president of Sycamore Machine, sit behind tables in the courtroom as they have throughout the three-week trial. Amanda closes her eyes and prays for a verdict that will provide for her and her children for the rest of their lives. Eric knows in his heart that Sycamore runs a safe factory and owes Amanda nothing.

The judge assumes the bench and calls the jury into the courtroom. The foreman stands and reads the verdict. "The jury finds for the plaintiff, Amanda Peterson, in the amount of $250,000."

No one is happy. Amanda's husband, Mark, had no life insurance; $250,000 is much less than Amanda thinks she needs to feed, clothe, and educate her four children. Eric is outraged because he is convinced that Sycamore Machine did nothing wrong. Each objects to the verdict. Each has options.

Motion for a New Trial

Either party can ask the judge to order a new trial before a new jury because the verdict is wrong. Since a jury has wide discretion to decide a case, unless the judge is also outraged by the result, this motion will probably be denied.

Motion for Judgment Notwithstanding the Verdict

Another approach is a motion for judgment notwithstanding the verdict. As with a motion for a new trial, you ask the judge to set aside the jury's verdict. However, rather than allow you to try the case again to a new jury, the judge enters the judgment he believes is appropriate. For example, if the judge concludes that Sycamore Machine did not negligently cause Mark Peterson's death and that the jury awarded Amanda $250,000 in sympathy, he could overrule the jury's decision and enter judgment for Sycamore Machine.

Because of the sanctity of jury verdicts and the risk of reversal on appeal, most judges are reluctant to substitute their judgments for those of juries. Though you may want to make this motion, if the judge believes that the jury's decision is unfair, the more likely result is a new trial.

Motion to Modify the Amount of the Verdict

Amanda Peterson is pleased that the jury found that Sycamore Machine is liable for Mark's death. Her objection is to the inadequate damages award. She could ask the judge to give her more money. The judge may also reduce the amount of damages in a case. Similar to a motion for a new trial or for judgment notwithstanding the verdict, this motion is based on the principle that the jury's damage award is not supported by the evidence or the law.

Motion for Reconsideration

Where the judge, not the jury, decides the case, you can file a motion for the judge to reconsider his decision. Since this motion depends upon the argument that the judge made a significant mistake, even if you're right, you probably won't win.

Settlement

In many cases, the parties discuss settlement after the trial. Settlement is particularly common where both sides recognize that the decision could be reversed on appeal and/or want to avoid additional time and expense. Settlement also often occurs in a jury case where the judge hints that he may grant a new trial or modify the damage award unless the parties resolve the case on their own. For example, if the judge is particularly sympathetic to Amanda Peterson, he could suggest that the jury verdict appears low and recommend that the parties resolve the case rather than force him to consider a motion for a new trial.

Appeal

Since the trial judge rarely grants a new trial or reconsiders his ruling, in most cases the only way to overturn a decision is through an appeal. You have a right of appeal to at least one court, often called a court of appeals. In some circumstances, if you don't like the decision of the first appellate court, you may be able to appeal to a second, usually known as a supreme court.

> "An appeal, Hinnissy, is where ye ask wan coort to show its contempt f'r another coort."
>
> —Mr. Dooley (Finley Peter Dunne)

The appellate court reviews the written briefs of the parties and the facts and law relating to the case. It then either affirms or reverses the lower-court decision. If it reverses, it may remand the case back to the trial court to hear more evidence.

Grounds for appeal fall generally into three categories. First, you can claim that the judge misapplied the law in rendering his decision, or misstated the law to the jury in the jury instructions. Because the court of appeals will consider legal errors without relying on the trial judge's interpretation, you should raise issues of law on appeal whenever possible.

A second basis for appeal is that the decision of the judge or jury is not supported by the facts. Appeals of factual issues are difficult because the court of appeals must rely to a large extent upon the findings of fact by the judge or jury. It will reverse only if the factual findings are "clearly erroneous."

A third category for appeal is that the judge improperly admitted evidence over your objection. Unlike a criminal case, you have little chance of winning an appeal on the basis of evidentiary mistakes by the trial judge. Even if he made mistakes, the court of appeals will probably find that the evidence was not important and that the judge's mistake was "harmless error."

Appeals take many months. The court reporter must prepare a transcript of the testimony. The appellant, the party filing the appeal, must then review the evidence and write a brief. The appellee responds with her own brief, and the appellant has the right to reply to the response. The judges on the court of appeals read the briefs and review the evidence and then often

Post-Trial Options

♦ New trial

♦ Judgment notwithstanding the verdict

♦ Modify the amount of damages

♦ Appeal

♦ Settle

allow the parties to argue their positions in oral argument. Finally, the judges write a decision. If you are a plaintiff waiting to collect your damages, sit tight because it could be a year or more before you get paid.

If the defendant loses and appeals, in some jurisdictions the plaintiff has the right to attempt to collect his damages during the appeal period unless the defendant posts a bond. A bond is a promise by a financial institution to pay the judgment if the defendant doesn't pay. Since a bond is often better than the right to execute on the defendant's assets, a plaintiff should try to force an appealing defendant to post a bond.

Getting Your Money

After the appeal process is complete and the case is over once and for all, a plaintiff has the right to execute on the defendant's assets if he doesn't pay. The sheriff takes whatever assets of the defendant he can find, including home, car, or boat, and sells them to satisfy the judgment. If the sheriff can't find sufficient assets, the plaintiff can subpoena the defendant's records and take his deposition to try to discover assets. Subject to exemptions that allow the defendant to keep some of his property, the plaintiff can take everything. Of course, since you can't get blood from a stone, if the defendant doesn't have the money, the plaintiff won't get paid.

ALTERNATIVE DISPUTE RESOLUTION: A BETTER WAY

Fast Fax manufactures fax machines and distributes them nationwide. It prides itself on its quality products and excellent service program. Though the fax machines are expensive relative to the competition, because of its quality and service, Fast Fax is extremely successful.

Beginning in 1990, Clear Image supplies component parts to Fast Fax under a five-year supply contract. During the first three years, there are no problems with the Clear Image components, and the relationship is fantastic.

In 1994, 35 percent of the fax machines begin to print unclear images. Fast Fax believes that the Clear Image components are defective. When Fast Fax confronts Clear Image about the lack of clarity, Clear Image argues that the components work perfectly and that there is a breakdown in the Fast Fax service program.

Tensions heighten as Fast Fax and Clear Image negotiate back and forth. The discussions degenerate into finger pointing. Finally, Fast Fax gets fed up and stops payment on a $750,000 check it sent to Clear Image. Clear Image is outraged and files a lawsuit.

Rather than embark on multiyear litigation, Fast Fax and Clear Image agree to mediate. In this process, they focus not only on the legal issues that drive the litigation, but also on the business issues that underlie their dispute. Clear Image needs money from the sale of the components. Fast Fax needs components that work. Rather than plod through the lawsuit, in the mediation they agree to implement a quality control program in which Fast Fax and Clear Image work together to ensure that all components are inspected and certified before they leave the Clear Image factory. Based on this quality assurance program, Fast Fax agrees to pay Clear Image $400,000, with more to come if the program succeeds. From this resolution, the parties move forward together in a prosperous business relationship. Fast Fax and Clear Image work out an efficient, cost-effective business solution to a business problem through a process known as alternative dispute resolution, or ADR.

Some say that it is a curse to be in litigation and be in the right. As the prior chapters demonstrate, litigation can be expensive, slow, and unpredictable. It can even be unfair. Moreover, it can tarnish a reputation and irrevocably damage relationships. Finally, the remedies available in litigation are often limited to a cash payment from one side to another.

For this reason, many have turned to ADR to manage their conflicts more effectively. ADR increases the involvement of the parties in the process, and reduces the role of lawyers and the legal and procedural battles on which they tend to focus. More important, a successful ADR proceeding can not only resolve a dispute, it can actually enhance a relationship by allowing the parties to explore new ways to work together to reach creative solutions to their problems.

Though ADR comes in many different forms, the two most common are mediation and arbitration. Each is appropriate in different circumstances. However, their goal is the same: to help the parties resolve their disputes more efficiently than in court.

Mediation

The fastest growing and most popular ADR technique is mediation. Mediation is a voluntary, nonbinding, structured dispute-resolution procedure in which an experienced third-party neutral assists the parties evaluate their claims and risks and reach resolutions that work for everyone. In this process, the parties and their lawyers meet with a trained mediator to discuss any options that may be available for solving their problem.

The mediation usually takes place in a conference room at the office of the mediator or one of the lawyers. It begins with a joint meeting. Each side states its position and listens to the opponent's side of the story. Thereafter, the mediator meets with the adversaries, sometimes individually and sometimes jointly, to attempt to narrow and focus the specific issues in the dispute and identify areas of common interest. Through this process, the mediator helps the parties create a solution that provides maximum benefit to both sides. The mediator focuses not on the legal rights of the parties that are judged in court but on their underlying business interests to fashion a business solution to what ordinarily is not a legal problem. As Don Reder, an experienced, non-lawyer mediator says at the start of every mediation, "We're not here to do justice, we're here to do business." There are no constraints on the issues that can be put on the table or the solutions that can be developed.

Why Mediation Works

Mediation works for many reasons. First, in mediation, the adversaries vent their feelings and hear the complaints of the other side. Each party can blow off steam and release frustrations. Consequently, the mediation gives the members of each side the feeling that they have "had their day in court," which is often necessary to allow them to get beyond their emotions to focus on their underlying interests. Moreover, through this venting, each party better understands where the opponent is coming from and any problems and concerns that affect the adversary's decision making. This face-to-face give and take, which infrequently occurs in litigation, enables the parties to better focus on resolving their dispute.

Second, and perhaps more important, is a trained mediator who facilitates discussion and helps develop and explore options. In mediation, everything that is said to a mediator is confidential and may not be disclosed to your opponent without consent. Consequently, parties typically disclose information to the mediator that they would not ordinarily disclose in a settlement conference. With the knowledge of this confidential information, the mediator is able to probe and suggest based on the collective knowledge that only he has to induce the parties to work out a solution that works for both of them. The flexibility of confidentiality allows the mediator to help the parties identify areas of common interest, which they could not do on their own.

Further, the flexibility of mediation helps it work. There are no procedural rules. The process can be modified in any way at any time. For example, the mediator may or may not evaluate the claims depending on whether it makes sense at any given time. Flexibility allows the parties to modify the process to take advantage of settlement opportunities.

Finally, in mediation, any solution is possible. Thus, unlike court, where solutions are usually limited to a cash payment from one side to the other, any resolution that suits the needs of the parties is appropriate. For example, an automobile accident case was settled in mediation when the defendant agreed to put up a plaque in honor of the deceased at the site of the accident. The surviving wife didn't need or want money. She wanted to honor her husband's life.

The dispute between Fast Fax and Clear Image was not resolved according to the legal rights of either party. For example, the settlement was not based on whether Fast Fax was right in stopping payment on the check. Rather, it arose out of Fast Fax's need for components, Clear Image's desire to sell components, and the mutual interests of both parties to implement an effective quality control program. This resolution helped both Fast Fax and Clear Image. More significant, it would not have been available in court. This ability to reach an infinite number of solutions greatly enhances the prospects of dispute resolution through mediation.

Selection of the Mediator

Because mediation is unstructured and open-ended, mediator selection is critical. You need a mediator with training and experience. Though many claim to be mediators, those without education and only a few cases under their belts generally lack the skills they need. Accordingly, ensure that your mediator has the experience to do the job.

Potential mediators run the gamut from the retired judge who may treat the mediation like a traditional court-sponsored settlement conference in which he announces within five minutes right and wrong and who should pay whom how much, to the unfocused, open-ended mediator who sees all the possibilities but never focuses the parties in a particular direction. Most mediators fall at some point on the spectrum between these two poles. The key to effective mediation is to find the mediator who is right for your dispute.

For example, if your adversary is unreasonable, fails to understand the weaknesses of his case, and needs an independent third party to give him a dose of reality, then you may want a judicial-minded mediator who will explain in no uncertain terms the facts of life to your opponent. This mediator can tell your opponent why he is wrong and strongly suggest the terms of a reasonable settlement. On the other hand, if legitimate issues are in dispute, each side has strengths, weaknesses, and risks in the litigation, and there are possibilities for an ongoing relationship, then a more broad-minded mediator can facilitate an exploration of possible nonlegal solutions to the dispute. However, every case is different, and different skills can be brought to each case. For this reason, before retaining a mediator, think carefully about the nature of the dispute, the legal and factual issues involved, whether you and your opponent have a reasonable good-faith interest in resolving the dispute, the nature of your past and possible future relationship together, and the possibilities for dispute resolution. Once you have conducted this analysis, you can focus more clearly on the type of mediator that will be best for you.

When Do You Mediate?

Generally speaking, you want to mediate as soon as possible. The longer you wait, the more time and money you spend on litigation. Since 95 percent of the lawsuits settle before trial anyway, there is no reason to prolong the litigation.

Moreover, mediation early in the process—before the parties become entrenched in their adversarial modes and more interested in winning than in resolving the dispute—may increase your chances of settlement. Litigation often takes on a life of its own, and mediation before this happens may be a smart strategy.

Notwithstanding the value of early mediation, mediation may not make sense until all parties are willing to consider settlement. Since mediation is voluntary and any resolution must be by agreement, it cannot be forced upon the parties. There must be some receptivity to the process from all sides.

Convincing Your Opponent to Mediate

Since mediation is relatively new in certain areas of the country, parties are often unwilling to mediate because they either don't trust or understand the process or because they consider an offer to mediate a sign of weakness. A number of points can be made to overcome objections raised by your adversary. These include:

- *The Wall Street Journal* reports that 85 percent of the business disputes mediated are resolved. Accordingly, most cases result in resolutions that are acceptable to all parties.

- Mediation is voluntary. You can leave at any time.

- Mediation achieves a nonbinding, consensual settlement.

- The mediation is completely confidential. None of the information disclosed in the mediation can be used in court.

- Mediation is fast.

- The parties pick the neutral mediator. They get a neutral they both trust.

- Legal fees and other litigation costs are reduced substantially.

- Clients devote much less energy and attention to mediation than litigation.

Arbitration

Unlike the nonbinding, structured negotiation process that is mediation, arbitration is a form of private judicial dispute resolution. Like mediation, it is governed by the agreement of the parties. For example, many business contracts, account agreements with stockbrokers, and insurance policies require arbitration of all disputes. The purpose of these arbitration clauses is to keep disputes out of court.

In arbitration, one or a panel of arbitrators hears evidence presented by each side. Thereafter, the arbitrator renders a decision as to who gets what. There is a winner and a loser. Though by agreement the resolution can be nonbinding, in most cases, the parties agree to a binding decision.

Though arbitration is much like court litigation, it tends to be quicker and more informal. For example, though discovery and, in particular, document production often occur, there is less of it conducted over a shorter period of time. Moreover, the arbitration hearing itself generally takes place not in a formal courtroom but in a conference room according to a schedule that is convenient for the parties and the arbitrator. For this reason, the arbitration can be more timely and efficient than court litigation.

Notwithstanding these potential benefits over court litigation, arbitration has come under fire in recent years. Though cost savings can be achieved, they often are insignificant relative to mediation. Moreover, like litigation, arbitrations can drag on. If the arbitrator allows broad discovery and does not impose limits on the hearings, arbitrations can take as long and cost as much as litigation.

An additional important factor in arbitration is that the rules of evidence generally do not apply. Rather, unless otherwise agreed by the participants, an arbitrator can hear any evidence, including evidence which is inadmissible in court, and decide a case based on any facts she considers appropriate. Since the right of appeal in arbitration is limited, the remedies for a bad decision by an arbitrator are few. Accordingly, arbitration may be more of a roll of the dice than court litigation. For these reasons, many believe that the potential benefits of arbitration are not worth the risks.

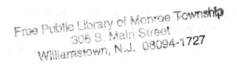

GLOSSARY

action   A shorthand name for a cause of action or lawsuit.

allegation   A statement by a party in a pleading of what he expects to prove.

alternative dispute resolution
Mediation, arbitration, minitrial, or some other nonjudicial procedure for resolving disputes.

authenticate   To establish that a piece of evidence is what a party claims it to be.

beyond a reasonable doubt   The burden of proof in a criminal case. A fact is proved beyond a reasonable doubt if every reasonable person would believe that it is true.

burden of proof   The standard by which the judge or jury determines the existence or nonexistence of a fact. Burdens of proof include "preponderance of the evidence" in a civil case, "clear and convincing" in a fraud case, and "beyond a reasonable doubt" in a criminal case.

case   A lawsuit.

cause of action   A set of facts or circumstances that give a party a right to a remedy such as money damages or an injunction. A claim.

claim   A right to payment or some other remedy. A cause of action.

class action   A lawsuit filed by an individual plaintiff on behalf of a large group of plaintiffs with similar claims.

clear and convincing   The burden of proof in certain civil causes of action, including fraud cases. It is more than a preponderance of the evidence but less than beyond a reasonable doubt. It is a firm belief or conviction.

clearly erroneous   The standard by which an appellate court reviews the findings of fact of a judge or a jury. A finding is clearly erroneous if it is contrary to the clear weight of the evidence.

code of professional responsibility
The rules written by the American Bar Association and adopted in most states to govern lawyer conduct and ethics.

collateral estoppel   The doctrine which precludes a party from litigating in a subsequent lawsuit facts that were in issue in a case.

compensatory damages   Monetary damages measured by the amount necessary to compensate a party for his loss.

competence   The doctrine that requires that a witness be both qualified and able to testify in court.

complaint   The document or pleading filed with the court to start a lawsuit that sets forth a cause of action.

counterclaim   A cause of action filed by a defendant against a plaintiff in response to a lawsuit.

court reporter   A trained professional who transcribes testimony in trials and depositions. The court reporter also prepares the transcript for appeal.

cross-claim   A cause of action filed by one defendant in a lawsuit against another defendant.

damages   A monetary remedy or award. Damages can be compensatory, the amount necessary to compensate a party for his loss, or punitive, the amount necessary to punish a party for his wrongful acts. Damages are general and special.

demonstrative evidence   Evidence which visually shows the facts a party is attempting to prove, including charts, maps, diagrams, etc.

de novo   Meaning "anew," the standard of review for legal issues on appeal. Appellate courts review legal issues as if they had not been decided in the trial court.

deposition   A part of the discovery process—taking testimony of a witness under oath before a court reporter prior to trial.

discovery   The pretrial process in which the parties investigate or discover all of the facts that relate to the case and narrow the issues for trial. Discovery procedures include interrogatories, requests for production of documents, depositions, and requests for admission.

document production   A part of the discovery process—the procedure by which the parties exchange documents relating to the lawsuit.

estoppel   A bar to assertion of a claim, defense or right.

evidence   Proof of facts presented at trial.

exhaustion of remedies   The principle that requires a plaintiff to avail himself of all required dispute resolution procedures before going to court.

general damages   Damages which natur-ally and necessarily flow from the wrongful act.

hearsay   An out-of-court statement offered to prove the truth of the fact contained in the statement.

injunction   An order by the court to do or not do something. Injunctions can be preliminary, which maintain the *status quo* until trial, or permanent, which are entered after a full trial on the merits.

in rem **jurisdiction**   Jurisdiction over property. *In rem* jurisdiction applies most often in suits over real estate.

interrogatories   Part of the discovery process—written questions one party serves on another that must be answered under oath and the penalty of perjury.

intervene   To join an ongoing lawsuit to protect a right or assert a claim.

jurisdiction   The authority of a court to hear and decide a case. The two principal jurisdictional questions are personal jurisdiction over the parties and subject matter jurisdiction over the case.

litigant   A party to a lawsuit.

litigation   A lawsuit.

motion   A request or application to the court seeking a ruling or order.

motion for directed verdict   A motion filed at the conclusion of the evidence requesting that the judge enter a verdict for the defendant because the plaintiff did not prove his case.

motion for judgment notwithstanding the verdict   A motion requesting the judge to enter a verdict that is contrary to the decision of the jury.

motion for new trial   A request that the judge void the jury verdict and order a new trial.

motion for protective order   A motion to limit or block discovery of certain facts.

motion for summary judgment   A motion that seeks judgment before trial on the grounds that there are no facts in dispute and that the case can be decided solely on the law.

motion in limine   A motion to block a party from introducing evidence in the trial.

motion to dismiss   A motion requesting the judge to dismiss a case based solely on the pleadings.

notice   In civil litigation, notice refers to advising an opponent of a lawsuit or particular matters in a lawsuit. For example, a party must send a copy of motions to his opponent to apprise him of the relief requested.

oath   An affirmation or attestation that a witness promises to tell the truth and that if she willfully fails to tells the truth, she can be punished for perjury.

party   A plaintiff, defendant, or other person who brought or against whom was brought claims in a lawsuit.

peremptory challenge   The right to challenge in jury selection any juror for any reason.

perjury   The crime of willfully giving false testimony under oath in a judicial proceeding.

personal jurisdiction   The power of the court over a defendant. A court cannot decide a case involving a defendant unless it has personal jurisdiction over him.

plaintiff   The party filing a lawsuit and asserting claims against the defendant.

pleading   A document containing the claims and defenses of the parties to a lawsuit.

prejudgment remedy   An attachment, garnishment or other procedure to obtain before trial an interest in the defendant's property that can be used to satisfy a judgment.

preliminary injunction   An injunction issued before trial that maintains the *status quo* between the parties until their rights can be determined at trial.

preponderance of the evidence The burden of proof in a civil case—more likely than not.

privilege   Privileged communications are those that cannot be disclosed in discovery or at trial without the consent of the person who holds the privilege.

pro se   Meaning "for himself," a *pro se* party appears on his own behalf without a lawyer.

process   The means by which a court exercises jurisdiction over a person and compels her

appearance in court. In civil litigation, the court issues a summons which requires a defendant to appear in court to respond to the allegations of the complaint.

punitive damages   Punitive or exemplary damages are awarded in addition to compensatory damages when the jury concludes that the defendant's conduct was willful and wanton and should be punished.

res judicata   Meaning "a matter judged," the doctrine that precludes a party from relitigating claims that were decided in a prior lawsuit.

requests for admission   A part of the discovery process—requests that a party admit the truth of particular facts or the application of law to facts.

rules of civil procedure   Rules that govern the prosecution and defense of civil litigation in state and federal courts.

rules of evidence   Rules that govern the admissibility of evidence in trials in state and federal courts.

service   The term for providing an opponent with notice of a motion, discovery request, or other matter in accordance with the rules of civil procedure. The most common method of service is by first-class mail.

service of process   The procedure for serving the summons and complaint that commences the lawsuit. The most common method of service of process is by personally delivering the summons and complaint to the defendant. There are alternative methods of service that should be checked in every case.

special damages   Damages that do not necessarily flow from the defendant's wrongful acts but that are reasonably foreseeable.

statute   A law passed by the legislature.

statute of limitations   A law which requires that claims be brought within a certain time period.

stipulation   An agreement by the parties that binds them throughout a lawsuit. For example, the parties may agree or stipulate that a court has jurisdiction to decide a particular matter or that certain facts are true for purposes of the litigation.

temporary restraining order   An injunction issued by the court without an evidentiary hearing and sometimes without notice to the defendant that freezes the *status quo* for no more than 10 days. A T.R.O. is generally entered in extreme circumstances.

third-party claim   A claim by a defendant against a party the defendant contends is liable for all or part of any damages for which the defendant is liable to the plaintiff.

transcript   An official, written, word-for-word recording of everything said in a trial or a deposition.

voir dire   Meaning "to speak the truth," the process by which the parties examine prospective jurors to determine whether they should be on the jury panel that decides the case.

waiver   The voluntary relinquishment of a known right.

work product   A privilege preventing an opponent from obtaining in discovery documents prepared in anticipation of litigation.

INDEX